SUCCESSFUL DOWNRIGGER FISHING

SUCCESSFUL DOWNRIGGER FISHING

Fred Olson

Winchester Press
Tulsa, Oklahoma

Copyright © 1981 by Fred Olson
All rights reserved

Library of Congress Cataloging in Publication Data

Library of Congress Cataloging in Publication Data
Olson, Fred.
    Successful downrigger fishing.

    Bibliography: p. 156
    1. Trolling (Fishing) 2. Fishing—Implements and appliances. 3. Sonar in fishing. 4. Fishes—Effect of water temperature on. I. Title. II. Title: Downrigger fishing.
SH457.7.045   639.02'028   81-10280
ISBN 0-87691-340-0   AACR2

Published by Winchester Press
1421 South Sheridan Road
P.O. Box 1260
Tulsa, Oklahoma 74101

Book design by Janice L. Merz

Photographs used in this book are by the author, unless otherwise indicated.

Printed in the United States of America

1 2 3 4 5 85 84 83 82 81

Contents

Introduction vii
 1. Don't Let a Fish Drown You! 1
 2. How to Talk to the Fleet 6
 3. Trolling Plans and Fish Migrations 12
 4. Ice-out in Lake Michigan 17
 5. Hunting Fish with a Thermometer 25
 6. How to Use Sonar Graphs and Flashers 46
 7. The Downrigger—a Trolling Machine 60
 8. The Trolling Trinity 79
 9. Trolling Tactics 90
10. Choosing the Right Lures 99
11. Fighting Fish with Rod and Reel 109
12. Salmon Trolling in the Salt 122
13. New Saltwater Frontiers 133
14. Mini-Rigging in Inland Lakes 142
Bibliography 156
Index 158

Introduction

Downriggers are devices that hold an angler's lure or bait at precisely the right trolling depth. They are in use in the Pacific and Atlantic, in the Gulf of Mexico, in the Great Lakes, in small and large inland lakes, and in impoundments. They are used for salmon, trout, char, bass, hybrid bass, walleye, sunfish, muskie, striped bass, tuna, marlin, sailfish, shark, grouper, dolphin, and many other species. Originally invented in the Great Lakes to solve trolling problems arising from the introduction of Chinook, coho, steelhead, and browns, they are now used in many parts of the world. Usually a downrigger will improve a fisherman's take anytime he wants to troll for a sustained distance in a specific water temperature zone.

When rigging down, a fisherman actually uses four trolling tools—a machine for raising and lowering a weight, a counter for recording depth, a weight, and a release mechanism for releasing the fishing line from the weight. These four related parts make up the downrigger. The device was invented because fish seek temperature habitats at depths where weighted lines do not troll efficiently. (See Figure 2.) When fishing it's important to decide where in the water the fish actually are and to present directly to that part of the water. But before downrigger equipment was developed, the fisherman could only make an educated guess about where his lure was being presented. The depth at which a lure trolled was affected by four variables: the length of the line, the line material and the weight of that material, the combined weight of the lure and the sinker, and the trolling speed. Various formulas were worked out that helped the guesswork. But the use of these formulas was never an easy science. Guesstimated fiddling with line, weight, and trolling speed fatigued and frustrated the fisherman. Each of the fishermen in Figure 1 knows that there are lake trout at 40 feet. They know this from sounding for the reef and taking fish, or from actually seeing both fish and reef on a sonar screen. But the only fisherman who can be certain that his lure is being presented at 40 feet is the fisherman with the down weight and downrigger cable. He's looking at a counter that marks down-weight depth. Of course his line will belly somewhat more than the right angle to the surface shown in the drawing, but only slightly more. The downrigger-equipped fisherman depends upon a trolled weight that actually tows the lure. The other two fishermen are towing line, weight, and lure, and each of these planes in the water as it adds weight. Moreover, rigging enough of the weighted lines to troll a significant swath results in tangles and snags when turning.

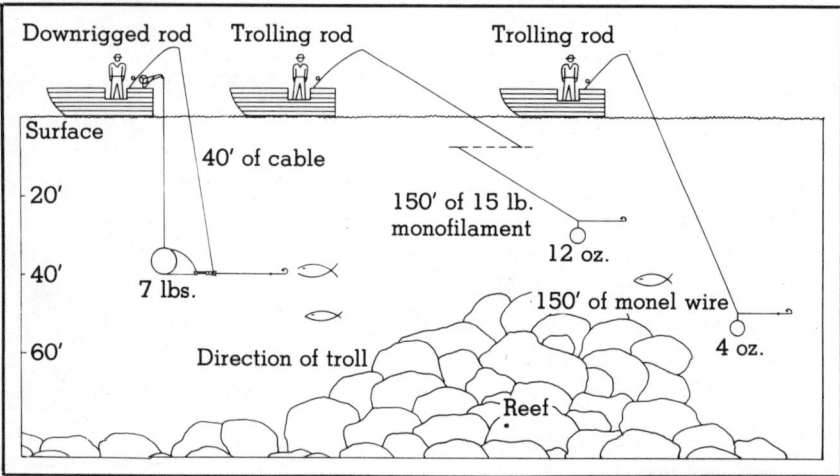

Figure 1. *Each of these fishermen hopes to troll for lake trout at 40-foot depth over and downwind from the 38-foot structure. Only one of them, the one with the downrigger, is trolling at exactly 40 feet. The two using trolling rods and weighted lines, despite reading the chart (Figure 2), are trolling at the wrong depth—the one using monofilament is too shallow; the one using wire is too deep. The down weight trolls forward at nearly right angles to the surface, while the monofilament and wire lines belly from the resistance of the water.*

Fishing Depth	With 15-lb. monofilament	With 20-lb. Monel wire
to 10 feet	4 oz.	—
to 20 feet	8 oz.	2 oz.
to 40 feet	12 oz.	4 oz.
to 60 feet	16 oz.	6 oz.
to 80 feet	20 oz.	8 oz.
to 100 feet	24 oz.	10 oz.

Figure 2. *Approximate weight requirements for trolling a flat line not rigged to a down weight (150 feet of line out—medium trolling speed). Reproduced courtesy of the Michigan Department of Natural Resources from Lievense, Stan: "Catching Great Lakes Salmon and Trout."*

Introduction

Although trollers had been disgusted with their inefficient equipment for many years, they limped along because they could take a fair number of fish in surface water and on the bottom. At the surface (anywhere within the first 30 feet), the planing variances of flat-line rigs can be tolerated and often guessed within reason. When fishing the bottom, fishermen bounced their weights off the rocks and sand, and they knew their lure was bouncing along somewhere behind the weight. But when the salmon came to the Great Lakes, and, during certain seasons, suspended at middle depths, the trollers found it very difficult to take them with regularity. Moreover, inspections by scuba divers and sonar viewers revealed that trolled lures were usually way out of range of the salmon's mouth. The fishermen didn't know either where their lures were trolling or where the fish were biting. It was the desire to fish the middle and to fish the top and the bottom of the Great Lakes with *more exact presentation,* that caused inventors there to create and manufacture the first downriggers.

Downrigger inventors were not thinking about pulleys and blocks and how to rig them efficiently. They were thinking about weights and lines. It became clear that heavy weights that towed lures made a more predictable profile in the water. It also became clear that wire or cable made it easier to raise and lower heavy weights and obviated line belly from trolling force. Heaving weights up and down and handling wire line with gloves caused trollers to use what men have used for centuries to take the strain off their backs—a pulley system. (See Figure 3.)

The Great Lakes fishermen who invented downriggers knew how distasteful it is to fight large fish whose mouths are "chained" to a down weight or window weight. Many of them remembered fighting lake trout (trophies once ranged up to about 40 pounds) on copper wire and a 10-pound weight. They wanted to avoid that unsporting method and develop a way of fighting fish on a free line. So they invented releases that allow the fish to detach the line from the down weight when it strikes. (See Figure 4.)

Probably downriggers, like the wheel, were invented and reinvented in many places. But combining the four parts of a downrigger into a unified, mass-produced machine was the contribution of Great Lakes manufacturers and inventors. Their efforts arose out of a creative desire to catch salmonids in the Great Lakes—a desire that inspired many homemade devices and created a market for factory-produced machines. Furthermore, the combination of sonar and temperature fishing with downrigged trolling arose out of this Great Lakes creativity and spread to other parts of the world.

SUCCESSFUL DOWNRIGGER FISHING

Figure 3. *The man on the left is hauling the weight up by main strength, and very awkwardly. His rope drags on the platform. His muscles hold the weight against the force of gravity. The man on the right is easily turning a pulley on a machine that holds the weight and raises it. A boom prevents the weight and cable from dragging on the platform. Hand-lining a weight from a boat is difficult work, and it isn't possible to mind several hand lines, fight a fish, and raise dangling weights without a machine.*

Introduction

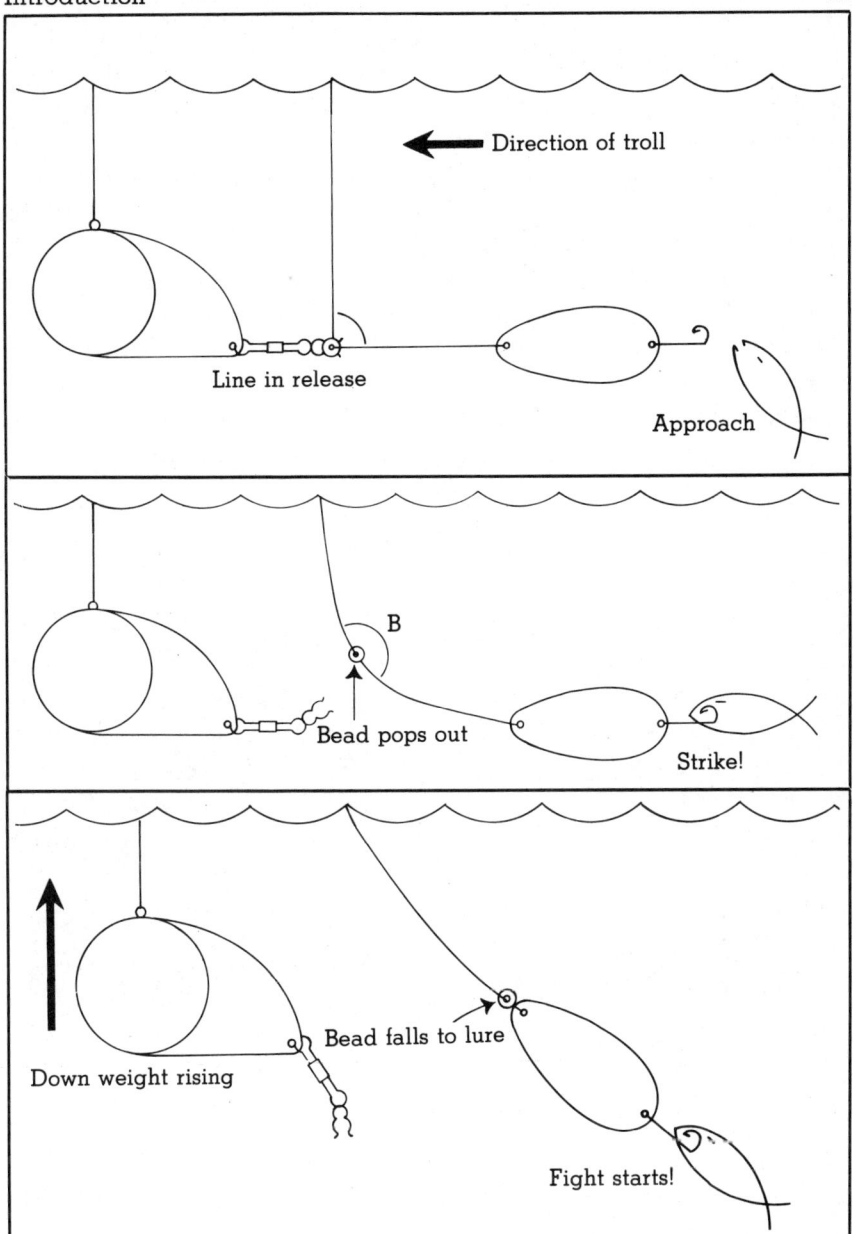

Figure 4. *The force of the fish's strike or the drag of the fish's body pulls the line from the release. Then the down weight is raised out of tangling way. Slack created by the right angle at A usually remains at B, but may be mostly straightened at C by the forward drift of the boat or by the fish's run. However, some slack may remain at C when the rod is picked up in the boat above the fish. In unusual circumstances a fish may strike hard from above and pop the release so fast that the rod will bend down instead of popping up. In that case, the fisherman should expect a tight line.*

Today it doesn't matter what depth a fish seeks for comfort and feeding. A downrigger will send a weight and a lure to that depth and keep it there. With sonar a fisherman can watch both his weight and the fish. (Although he probably won't be able to see his lure on the sonar screen, he knows where it is in relation to the weight.) With temperature probes riding at the same depth as the downrigger weight, the fisherman can tell where to look with his sonar and where to troll his lure. Furthermore, every fish taken with a downrigger is fought on a nonweighted line; the downrigger allows the fisherman to give the fish a sporting chance. (For a complete view of a downrigger, see Figure 15.)

So this is a book about an improved trolling method. It's also a book

A steelhead being played on a Berkley rod with Penn 209 reel; Proos downriggers on the gunwale. This was a grand slam day: steelhead, brown, lake trout, coho, and Chinook. (Courtesy Michigan Travel Commission.)

about an improved fish-hunting method called temperature fishing. Temperature fishing, which developed hand in hand with downrigger trolling in the Great Lakes area, confuses fishermen. The basis for temperature fishing is that fish move through water as temperature changes, and they are active in the water they inhabit when it's not abnormally warm or cold. From this base biologists have created preferendums giving the minimum and maximum temperatures at which fish are active. Because activity includes feeding and because the preferendums usually give one midrange, temperature fishermen jump to the conclu-

Introduction

sion that they can guarantee the fish will hit if they can find the ideal water temperature. Unfortunately this is not the purpose of temperature fishing, nor is it the theme of this book. Thermometers are used to find fish *habitat*. Sonar is used to find which parts of the usable habitat are inhabited. Downriggers are used to present the lures. They must still be presented with skill. They must move in a way that interests fish. They may remind the fish of something edible. They should be a color that's visible at the depth presented. They should be trolled at the proper speed. But there's no magic temperature that will relieve us of the burden of using our brains and experience. So the purpose of the thermometer is to help us find fish habitat. It improves our chances of finding fish. Downrigger fishing is the union of three new methods—the use of thermometers to locate fish habitat (the covert birds use), the use of sonar to find fish within the habitat (the dog that finds the birds within the covert), and the use of a trolling machine to present lures (the shotgun that sends the pellets). Fishermen still have to aim the gun, select the shot weight and pattern, and pull the trigger.

In addition to reading this book, the serious student of trolling should read my stream-fishing book, *Exciter Fishing*. It fully presents the general biology needed for understanding how to extend one's senses into the fish's water medium—how to think as fish think.

SUCCESSFUL DOWNRIGGER FISHING

1
Don't Let a Fish Drown You!

Whether you mini-rig in small lakes or far out in a salt or inland sea, you're taking some risk. In water, humans are exposed. Water temperature is seldom high enough to keep the inner organs warm. In midsummer in Lake Superior, even if you're only three-quarters submerged you can die in about ten to twenty minutes. Small, cold trout lakes, even though land is nearby, are equally dangerous.

Moreover, our vulnerable, warm-blooded, hairless bodies are led into danger by our passions. "Coho fever" is a real disease. Why did my son and I continue to fish for muskie after lightning struck a tree and blew it apart only 20 feet from the bay where I was standing up in the boat to cast? "Because we had had one on!"

It was night. David continued to row me over the miniature whitecaps illuminated by the lightning. I continued to cast my Giant Pikie Creek Chub upward to let the wind sail it over the weedbed I was fishing. My blood was up! The exhilaration of that moment returns to me as I write, but I shake my head wondering why I kept a fifteen-year-old boy rowing in that storm. As the storm's fury increased, we sobered enough to beach our boat and walk across the peninsula through the woods to shelter.

Once while fighting a steelhead from a 14-foot boat in Lake Superior at the protected mouth of the Misery River, I motored after the fish, which in run after run peeled line from the reel. Suddenly boat, fisherman, and fish were out of the lee of Fourteen Mile Point and in the teeth of an oncoming front of driving wind and mounting waves. I cut the line, but the boat had only a 5-horse engine and couldn't take a heading in the following waves, which swept over the transom, setting all gear awash. Trembling with fear, I turned the bow into the wind and adjusted the spitting water-soaked engine in tension against the waves so that course was held, but no way made. The winds and waves slowly carried fisherman and boat backward to a hazardous landing in the sandy surf. Having survived my passions I built a fire under a hemlock behind the beach dunes. The fish, at home under the whitecaps, swam off with the only piece of lost gear—my Dardevle.

When the coho came from the Pacific Ocean to the Great Lakes, a fevered fleet of trolling fishermen defied U.S. Coast Guard cutters and planes in the teeth of a Lake Michigan storm. On September 23, 1967, seven drowned near Frankfort and hundreds of boats were wrecked in the surf between Empire and Elberta. The monument to their death is the eternal vigilance of downrigger captains in all waters. The U.S. Coast Guard Auxiliary textbook *Boating Skills and Seamanship* (7th edition) says that hunters and fishermen have been involved in approximately 24 percent of all boating fatalities because they "use their boats as a form of conveyance."

A boat beached during the September storm in which seven persons drowned near Frankfort, Michigan. Note the homemade downrigger lying across the gunwales. (Courtesy Michigan Department of Natural Resources, Information and Education Division.)

Don't Let a Fish Drown You!

A captain's first passion should be for his boat. It's not just transportation! Working the boat should be as much pleasure as fishing. "Boating fever" is the counterirritant for "coho fever." Please, reverently say "Sir" to the captain who has both diseases!

The 1967 "coho fever" was incubated in the fall of 1966 when fishermen from all over the Midwest caught their first salmon jacks in Michigan's rivers. In the fall of 1967, 10- and 20-pounders were being taken and fishermen were arriving in one small Michigan shore city at the rate of 10,000 to 15,000 per day during the week and 40,000 on weekends. They slept in their boats and cars. Lines formed at restaurants. Filling stations that usually sold a few hundred gallons of gasoline a day pumped thousands. Nurses hung a sign over one hospital emergency room reading "Welcome Coho Fishermen." Lures were sold out. A fisherman pleaded with a doctor removing a lure from his wife's ear: "Careful, Doc, that's the last one of those baits I've got!" Hot lures sold for $10 under the counter. Because of the popularity of silver flatfish, aerosol cans of silver paint sold out even in inland cities.

In town, trollers' behavior amused the overworked authorities, but at sea their behavior frightened the Coast Guard. The lake had been unusually calm during August and September, and fishermen were overly bold. Small rubber rafts, canoes, and 14-foot cartoppers were sighted 7 miles at sea. On Saturday, September 23, there were over 1,000 small boats between the Platte and Manistee rivers. By 8:00 a.m. the Point Betsie and Frankfort Coast Guard Stations had raised the triangular red daytime Small Craft Warning pennant to signal that winds could become as high as 33 knots. As wind velocity increased, fishermen could see the dark clouds and increasing waves that National Weather Service radio transmissions had predicted. The Coast Guard stations sent cutters that broadcast warnings on their hailers, but many fishermen shook their fists because the cutters zigzagging between the tightly packed boats circled over their trolling lines. Hailer-equipped airplanes flew through the darkening clouds making out like God shouting from heaven, but only a few of the coho-maddened fleet headed for port in time. The sea, driven by winds from the southwest, continued to rise, and by 2:30 p.m. waves outside Platte Bay were 25 feet. Coast Guard sailors reported that some do-or-die fishermen trolled from their swamped boats while being towed to shore. Inside the bay it became obvious that beaching or running into the Platte River mouth, where there's adequate draft for most craft ranging up to 20 feet, was in order. But many fevered fleet members tried to run back to their cars and trailers at Frankfort and Empire. Those running to Frankfort came around the lee of Point Betsie into the full fury of the storm. Some compounded their errors by running close to the coastline, where the wind drove them into the surf.

The Coast Guard was already directing a search-and-rescue mission. Afterward two station commanders—Bosun's Mate 1st Wesley E. Davis, Frankfort, and Bosun's Mate 1st Wilbur McVay, Point Betsie—were commended for resourceful action. Cutters at sea were joined by Sheriff's Boat Patrol members who towed boats, sirens screaming, down highways from many adjacent inland cities and counties. Rescue workers were joined by helicopters, planes, and sea-wise captains recruited into a cooperating armada directed by marine radio transmitted by the Coast Guard. Command order prevailed as Coast Guard officers directed sweeps of the sea for overboard fishermen. Many were plucked out of the water as helicopters hovered over them. Ambulances brought the exposed and injured from docks to hospital emergency rooms. Hearses brought seven to funeral parlors.

While switchboards were jammed with emergency calls and clergymen informed bereaved survivors, the Coast Guard was already summarizing field reports for a board of inquiry. The board, under the chairmanship of Captain Lester A. Levine, sat in the Manistee County Courthouse during the second week of October. Survivors testified with awe and disbelief to the fury of the winds and the waves they had experienced. On October 12 in a front-page story the *Benzie County Patriot* said: "Under the gentle but insistently probing questions of the board, it developed that all the boating parties which were to number seven victims had made an identical sequence of mistakes. (1) They had all failed to seek out weather information or had ignored it. (2) They had failed to take early alarm at the storm rapidly approaching from the southwest. (3) They had finally tried to beach their boats through heavy surf.

"One other fact that board carefully noted. No man who drowned was wearing a lifejacket, although in each case his boat was equipped with them."*

Homemade downriggers rusted on the wrecked boats that littered the beaches. I saw my first one on a day in late November while casting the surf north of Otter Creek. It was a strange assemblage of discarded pulleys and tubular steel. The down weight, still attached to the rusting

---

*If a captain smells grease burning in a skillet in the galley stove he'll investigate, then pass out the lifejackets. If he says: "Lifejackets, everyone!" put the damned thing on and tie it down. Do it even though you saw the hamburger grease smoking. Why? Because the captain wants that detail out of the way, so if a real emergency develops he can respond to the problem without having to instruct several confused, underdressed people.

cable, lay in the bottom of the wooden boat. It was a piece of railroad iron with a ring through a centered hole. The boat was long enough, about 20 feet, to have weathered the storm that cast it high upon the beach. Sand had blown halfway up on the gunwale. There's no knowing who put that downrigger together, but it's wise to remember that one of the world's first downrigger captains went aground during the September storm that launched the Great Lakes sports salmon fishery. From that time downrigger captains have prided themselves on nautical safety.

2
How to Talk to the Fleet

A stream fisherman is the captain of his waders, with the responsibility for getting ashore with a dry butt. A downrigger fisherman is the captain of a boat with a jillion responsibilities. But he's not alone. He's part of one of the world's most friendly groups—the fleet at his home port. "How about it, buddy?" your CB will blat, and you'll respond with more verbiage than you want to use to the redhead in the blue Bayliner who's already taken two coho at 23 feet with J-Plugs.

Actually, there are two grades of sportfishing captains—charter captain and owner captain. A charter captain is licensed, and has passed stringent tests. When you're a passenger on the boat of either, it's up to you to mind the captain. You may be on a fishing party, but according to Coast Guard usage and boating tradition, captains have responsibilities; passengers have duties.

Among the friends in your home fleet there are usually members of the Coast Guard Auxiliary (CGA). Some of them have downrigger equipment, and all of them will help you select emergency gear and get your craft straight with the law. CGA members have no police power. They have the right, if invited, to inspect your boat for compliance with safety law—a Courtesy Examination. If they find violations, they cannot cite you. If you're not in reasonable compliance with the law, they'll refuse to issue you a current Courtesy Examination decal. But not to worry! They'll come back for another friendly inspection when you call to say that you're

How to Talk to the Fleet

in compliance. As a Coast Guard cutter crew approaches a prudently operated boat, they'll usually wave the captain on when they see the Courtesy Inspection decal. That saves everyone taking time for an official inspection boarding.

Fishing all the water there is in a lake or ocean requires boat-to-boat cooperation. In this book you'll learn how to find productive water by using a thermometer and a graph, but the buddy system is another important tool in downriggering.

In nearly every port there are downrigger organizations. In Michigan ports there's always a member of the Michigan Steelhead & Salmon Fishermen's Association within easy hail and a chapter meeting place within reasonable driving distance. The Ontario Charter Boat Association is the fleet's friend in Ontario. Lake Superior Steelhead Association members are part of the fleet at Duluth, Minnesota. Erie Downriggers, Inc. is an active 500-member group at the port of Erie, Pennsylvania.

The fleet in Illwaco Harbor, Washington, where salmon fishermen enter the Columbia River to troll the Pacific. Learn how to communicate with the fleet, and you'll learn how to be a fisherman.

"Erie Downriggers was organized to help members catch fish," says Bob Chandler, Erie Tourist and Convention Bureau director. When downrigger-equipped fishermen first went out of the port of Erie to take salmon, they were a few separate captains searching a gigantic amount of water. Most had graphs, thermometers, and downriggers and the know-how to operate them. But the schools of salmon changing location from Presque Isle Bay to shoals far out in the lake eluded them. Nearly everyone was fishing water of the correct temperature, but the fish did not fill every foot of that water. A proper organization of the searching-trolling ships and effective two-way communication were needed. In January of 1977, fifty Erie downrigger captains met and set up a salmon tracking steering committee, headed by Captain Ted Halgren, an Erie architect. The committee created a map for captains to refer to when calling ship to ship. The map divided all Pennsylvania waters into numbered square-mile grids over accurate bottom contour. The committee also appointed key captains responsible for communicating by radio and eliciting further radio communication. Buoys were constructed for these captains to drop when they located salmon schools. These actions created a fleet that the public and other downrigger fishermen could identify. By mid-July, the fleet had found five separate schools of salmon about 7 miles north of Shorewood over two underwater "mountains." These "mountains" are about 40 feet below the surface of the water near a point where water depth drops swiftly to 110 feet—a place salmon like.

On shore, communication was enhanced by establishment of a hotline financially sponsored by John Smith, manager of the Howard Johnson restaurant. As more captains fished over the "mountains," a common taking pattern was identified. Salmon were taking lures in 65- to 80-foot depths off the north slopes of the "mountains." This information, which improved trolling productivity and reduced gasoline consumption, resulted in many all-hands limits. When the action, which continued for several weeks, was broken by violent storms that dispersed the fish, fleet members, motivated by the success of previous cooperation, trolled in radio concert until the schools were relocated. "This is our fleet, and we continue to help each other," says Fred Abbot, a charter Erie Downrigger member and the 1980 president, from the wheel of his boat, the *Bacchus*.

Radio communication is the grapevine of a fleet-civilian band for prudently tempered fishing chatter; the marine band is for navigation. Correct nautical speech and an understanding of radio electronics will help you make intelligent ship-to-ship and ship-to-shore conversation.

Originating messages on your boat radiotelephone is very different from playing the radio in your parlor. A radiotelephone originates broadcasts over its own transmitter, so it's a radio station. The radio in your parlor monitors messages broadcast from a distant and separate radio station. The captain must be licensed by the Federal Communications Commission if he has a radiotelephone on board. And that's why you must have the captain's permission to speak on the marine band.

Radio stations can be equipped with carriers to send pulsations measured on a frequency spectrum from 100 to 10,000 kHz or .1 to

10,000 MHz. Hz is the abbreviation for Hertz, which means cycles per second. M stands for million; k for thousand. MHz is the abbreviation for megahertz, which means 1,000,000 cycles per second; kHZ is the abbreviation for kilohertz, which means 1,000 cycles per second. So the frequency of the pulsations emitted by a carrier is expressed in both kHz and MHz. (Divide kHz by 1,000 to get MHz.) These pulsations can be amplified to make the peaks higher and the valleys lower—amplitude modulation, AM. The distance between a peak/valley and the successive peak/valley can also be changed by amplification—frequency modulation, FM. The federal government regulates certain middle-range frequencies. The government states the purpose for which these frequencies may be used and the way they may be modulated. It has designated the frequencies from 155 MHz through 162 MHz for marine usage only. They're called marine-band VHF-FM (very high frequency–frequency modulation).

Marine VHF-FM has a range of about 50 miles and designates the only official (Coast Guard–used) marine radiotelephone communication on the Great Lakes. Marine VHF-FM is also used on the American coasts up to the 50-mile range. On the coastal waters certain AM frequencies are also used because ships travel beyond the 50-mile range of VHF-FM. The AM coastal waters watch channel for distress, safety, and calling is 2182 kHz-AM. The VHF-FM Great Lakes watch channel for distress, safety, and calling is 156.8 MHz VHF-FM, or Channel 16. On coastal waters, the Coast Guard will send and receive on both watch frequencies. So a Great Lakes radio can be used up to 50 miles on coastal waters, but an AM set from coastal waters will not receive Great Lakes transmissions. All marine-band radiotelephones in the 156 to 162 MHz band must be equipped to send and receive on Channels 16, 6, and at least one other working frequency. This is the touchstone for short-range marine communication.

A Citizen's Band (CB) radiotelephone is not a good aid to navigation. In the first place, the Coast Guard station in the area where you're trolling may not be able to hear your CB transmission even if they are monitoring Channel 9, and they're not required to monitor it. The reason the Coast Guard may not be able to hear you is that CB does not have a good range on VHF-FM and it's more vulnerable to atmospheric interference. Also, CB is an informal party line. If someone is "playing" with that party line, he may not yield quickly enough to make it possible for you to transmit an emergency message. It's like having your house burning while the second party on a two-party line refuses to yield so you can call the fire department. Although all CB stations are asked to monitor Channel 9 at all times, this is a request and not a command. You may send a Mayday on Channel 9, and most of the boats in your reception area may be listening to a blonde on another channel.

Do not jump to the conclusion that a VHF-FM radiotelephone is a high-power station. The average ship-to-ship range is about 10 to 15 miles; the expected ship-to-shore range is 20 to 30 miles. The FCC limits marine-band transmitter power to 25 watts and requires that each station be able to reduce power to 1 watt for short-range communication. Because captains are using short-range instruments, it's important they work well. The receivers should have superior sensitivity and adjacent channel rejection.

The nameplate of a VHF-FM receiver may give an indication of its sensitivity. In these receivers the sensitivity norm is the number of microvolts required to produce 20 decibels (dB) of quieting. The better the sensitivity, the smaller the microvolt number—.5 is better than 2.0. But some manufacturers escape cross-comparative shopping by specifying sensitivity in terms other than 20 dB.

Adjacent channel rejection is a specification that indicates a receiver's ability to reject unwanted signals and accept the selected channel. This is expressed on the nameplate as a negative number of dB. The larger the number, the better the adjacent channel rejection—minus 70 dB is better than minus 50 dB.

Marine-band radiotelephones are an aid to navigation for the following reasons:

1. The Coast Guard and all marine-band-equipped craft are monitoring Channel 16 at all times, and the FCC polices the usage of that frequency to prevent "party line" foul-ups.

2. Therefore your Mayday followed by a statement of your position will be monitored. That's a high probability.

3. In the case of explosion or a hull-rending collision, you can give a Mayday position with a high hope it'll be heard even if you immediately go down or leap away from the heat into the water.

4. All licensees are required to monitor Channel 16. This is a command, not a request. Therefore if you send a Mayday on marine band, there's a good chance that a nearby boat will immediately start toward you.

5. The local Coast Guard station and the National Weather Service will cooperate to give hazardous-weather warnings through Channel 16.

6. The National Weather Service broadcasts taped weather messages that are updated every three to six hours on a VHF-FM marine-band channel.
7. Marine-band radiotelephones have an Intership Safety Channel, Channel 6. The watch officer of a large ship could, for example, use that channel to warn you of immediate danger.

If you can walk on water you won't need these safety factors, and you could downrig with a CB set only. It's less expensive! But a downrigger captain on big water is both fishing and navigating. Unlike a commercial fisherman cooperating with a small number of other ships that fish reasonably regular hours, the downrigger captain fishes with a larger fleet whose members are more fluid in participation times. So a downrigger captain needs a separate radio for each task—navigation and fishing.

If a captain in distress elects to use radiotelephone, he may initiate transmission by saying one of three words:

1. Mayday—the distress signal. This top-priority message indicates grave, immediate danger and requests immediate assistance.
2. Pan (pronounced *pahn*)—the urgency signal. This signals that a vessel or person is in jeopardy. It might mean "man overboard."
3. Security (pronounced *say curity*)—The safety signal. This signals a navigation hazard (perhaps a boat going aground) or a meteorological warning (perhaps a tidal wave).

Transmission of any of these three signals establishes precedence over other communication. *Listen. Do not transmit. Get ready to help.*

There are ten steps to follow when sending a distress signal. Not to worry—no one is keeping score. The Coast Guard radio operator will try to establish all the facts, but he'll already dispatch assistance while talking with you. Remember to give the name of your boat, your position, the nature of your distress, and the assistance required. The ten steps are listed in the U.S. Coast Guard Auxiliary publication *Boating Skills and Seamanship*.

The major downrigging purpose of CB is to help your "good old buddies" find fish. This can be done in the vernacular. Unfortunately, CB communication is often overly verbose and lacking in precision. The importation of games motorists play with "Smokey the Bear" and truck drivers' needs to ventilate their over-the-road feelings into marine traffic has further screwed up CB transmission. Few know and many have forgotten that there are Procedure Words (listed in *Boating Skills and Seamanship*) that reduce transmission time and nervous chatter.

Welcome to the fleet. We hope we've helped you talk to us. *Out!*

3
Trolling Plans and Fish Migrations

"The most important tool in fishing is the thermometer," says Joe Hughes, public relations director for Rebel. "If I were asked to choose one tool among graph, downrigger, color gauge, and oxygen gauge, I'd take the thermometer." In Chapter 2 we discussed radio—the tool used in the buddy system of locating fish. In this chapter we're going to talk about locating fish through species knowledge. In the first part of Chapter 5, we'll discuss locating fish through knowing water physics. In the second part of Chapter 5, we'll talk about how to use a thermometer. It sure takes a long time to get around to our most important tool!

Why does it take so long? "You have to know where to stick the thermometer," the doctor said to the student nurse as he removed it from the patient's ear. Even in an inland lake there's a lot of water out there. After you've found the water the fleet uses, and the water a species uses for feeding and spawning migrations, and the water that has the correct physical state, you're still not certain the water beneath you has the correct temperature. But you're ready to put the thermometer into the water. Let's continue getting ready by discussing migration patterns of salmon, trout, and char in the Great Lakes, with the Michigan sides of Lake Michigan and Lake Huron as specific examples. If you fish an ocean or an inland lake, you'll have other migration patterns to consider. For the Pacific Ocean you can get good information from Squire and Smith's *Anglers' Guide*. For the Atlantic read Freeman and Walford's *Anglers' Guide*.

Trolling Plans and Fish Migrations 13

Salmon porpoising near Manistee Harbor, Michigan. "The fish are laughing behind the trollers' backs," explains Gill Clarke, Michigan Travel Bureau photographer. (Courtesy Michigan Travel Commission.)

In Lakes Huron and Michigan we catch two Pacific salmon, Chinook and coho; two trout, steelhead and browns; and one char, lake trout. There are a few Atlantic salmon (a trout) from experimental plants, and once in a while someone takes one. There are more and more pink salmon in the upper part of Lake Michigan, but so far they haven't been caught in significant numbers by downrigger fishermen.

Chinook, coho, browns, and steelhead are anadromous fish, so they make two major migrations: from streams as parr into Big Water (salt or fresh), where they migrate in search of feed; then after their feeding season back into their birth stream to spawn. They are caught during their feeding migration in Big Water and during their spawning migration in streams. Lake trout (a char) are not anadromous, that is, they do not spawn in streams. It's true that they sometimes run into streams at their spawning time, but this is atypical behavior. We fish for lake trout during their feeding time and when they are on spawning shoals.

All of these fish belong to the salmon-trout subfamily called Salmonidae. They are discussed in complete detail in *Exciter Fishing*. From reading that book you can learn how to catch them in streams during their spawning fast, and how to identify them and tell them apart. More information about each is in the junior encyclopedia in the back of the book.

In winter, immature coho follow alewives into the southern end of Lake Michigan. Therefore, they are the predominant fish caught during early-spring trolling beginning in late March. They run from 1 to 3 pounds. Although Chinook do not congregate like coho, there are many planted in southern Michigan, and they're caught with coho. They may run from 10 to 12 pounds, and there'll be a few larger ones that did not make a previous fall spawning run. Small steelhead, brown trout, and lake trout are also caught.

The "bite" gets good as the water warms to 40 degrees. This warming occurs in shallow water 3 to 10 feet deep along the beach and may, if the sun is warm, extend out to depths of 30 or 40 feet.

During the early spring, coho are concentrated south of Saugatuck. They start northward as the ice melts and the water warms. Fishermen from South Haven notice increasing concentrations; then they arrive off Grand Haven.

More Chinook take as the water warms, but few of them migrate. We do know that some Chinook migrate because before Wisconsin wildlife managers planted their own Chinook, they received a migration from Michigan plants. The same thing is true for browns. Most of them stay put, but before Michigan planted browns, there was an appreciable migration from Wisconsin plantings. So although browns and Chinook do not migrate as much as coho, there are many wanderers in each species.

Lake trout are also taken in southern Michigan waters during early spring. Most of them are small, but some large ones ranging up to 20 pounds may become active enough to take. The lake trout are not usually taken in great number until about three weeks after the coho begin to take.

Because they migrate, coho planted in Michigan waters of Lake Huron swim to Canadian nets. An annoyance! Chinook, on the other hand, stay put to be caught by the taxpayers who planted them. Coho winter near Sarnia, Ontario, providing early-spring fishing there. On the Michigan shore, spring fishing begins in late March with lake trout. In Lake Huron, Michigan's first spring browns and steelhead are usually between Au Gres and Tawas City. Lake trout and browns are taken from season's beginning at Port Austin.

The northern ports of Lake Michigan usually get their first significant fishing about May 15 to June 1. Whatever the variance in season from northern to southern ports may be, it's safe to say that the northern opening lags. The northern ports can be roughly defined as north of Muskegon–Grand Haven. This is a logical boundary, because two warm-water rivers, the Muskegon and the Grand, flow into the cities that have

Trolling Plans and
Fish Migrations   15

their names.

As spring fishing ends (about the end of May), there may be a lull in fishing takes because fish disperse. All the lake waters are warming, there's a much wider area of comfortable water for the fish, and assembly areas such as thermoclines and thermal pockets are not definitely formed. This is a period for searching far and wide with the thermometer down at all times.

Late May and early June usually see the beginning of summer fishing in Lake Michigan. Chinook begin to take in appreciable numbers. They take in the place where they lie sluggish in colder weather. Or, in other words, they don't seem to follow the smelt migrations to stream mouths, then turn away from shore to move toward the first thermoclines.

As early thermoclines form, forage fish gather in comfortable water (often 50 to 55 degrees F.). Steelhead and browns may be slightly above the forage fish in 55- to 65-degree water, and coho and Chinook may be at the same level. The lakers will be deeper in colder water. This formation is an ideal pattern, and the fish and fishermen have to work out the actual daily development. Use the graph and thermometer creatively and share information by radio.

As the season progresses, the thermocline gets deeper and the fish larger. Chinook and coho may move into Michigan waters from Illinois and Wisconsin. Chinook will be at 120 feet, and in late August they'll begin their spawning migrations to river mouths. At the same time browns will move toward shore. Steelhead that make fall runs into streams to overwinter will wait a few weeks, then begin their migration.

In September and October the sunlight slants and the lake cools. Many sexually mature Chinook are already in the streams spawning. Most of them will have left their lake feeding grounds. Coho will be migrating riverward behind the Chinook and may be continuing their migration away from lake feeding grounds into November. Trolling for them and for fall-run steelhead and browns off river mouths may be productive from October through November.

The lake trout spawning migration from deep lake waters to shallow shoals near shore may begin as early as Labor Day. Trolling over the shoals may be productive into late November.

This general knowledge of feeding and spawning migration routes will help downrigger captains plan. In the Pacific Ocean where coho, Chinook, and steelhead also live, the migration patterns for them have the same general form—longer migrations for coho within the ocean and not such long migrations, as a rule, for Chinook; a fall return from ocean feeding to streams for spawning by Chinook and coho and for overwintering by steelhead. Coho from as far north as Oregon winter in southern California and start migrating as ocean waters warm. (They are a more significant fishery in summer north of Fort Bragg than south.) How far coho migrate to the south and what they feed on in winter is not known, according to Joe Lesh, a California fish and game biologist. Salmon running out of Puget Sound into the ocean used to turn north toward Alaskan net. An effort has been made to develop "left-turning" salmon. Until that biological challenge arose, most Chinook in the Sound area migrated north and most coho south. Chinook provide year-round fishing in the Inside Passage, which lies between the Alexander Archipelago and the coast from Seattle to Skagway. In the other oceans and in large inland lakes and impoundments, these lessons can be applied with specific reference to season, water conditions, and species.

Following is a summary of the spawning and feeding migration patterns that Michigan captains on Lakes Huron and Michigan use to plan their trolling year.

In the early spring the taking fish are near shore—often in river current influence. After chasing smelt, the coho, lakers, and browns will move toward deeper water where Chinook are waking up. After that, temperature hunting for thermal pockets and thermoclines and along points and bars will be productive. In late summer, thermometer hunting should be plotted between deep water and river mouths. In early fall, temperature-hunting trolling trips should be planned between river mouths and within river-current influence. In late fall, trolling the thermometer over spawning shoals and deep drop-offs near the shoals could be a good plan. During November it's time to put the boat up and head upstream to drift-fish for overwintering steelhead. In some streams, you may find late-run coho or browns.

4
Ice-out in Lake Michigan

The southern ports of Lake Michigan are pleasant places to begin trolling after ice is out. Because the tip of Lake Michigan hangs into the southern warmth of Indiana, the season may begin just a little earlier there than in other Great Lakes ports. The coho that migrate into these "southern" waters provide good trolling along the lake shore as the surface water warms toward 43 degrees. I started the 1978 season there, two weeks after ice was out, with Charter Captain Don Torba, Charter Captain Joe Kimmerly, and Captain Don Goodwillie, Jr. These men began fishing while downriggers were being invented. They bought from the first downrigger manufacturers and based their fishing on the temperature methods taught by Stan Lievense, natural resources manager for the Michigan Travel Bureau. They illustrate the Great Lakes methods developed for taking salmon, trout, and char—methods now used in inland lakes and impoundments and in oceans.

Captain Goodwillie was remounting a Plath downrigger on the transom of his 26-foot Stamas, the *Sue-Ya,* when I arrived at the dock in Black River Harbor at South Haven. Goodwillie fished 185 times in 1977 and took 1,026 fish. He'd fished three times this spring, he explained as he shook hands, "with a bag of only fifty-one fish." I managed to be comically sympathetic and was invited aboard.

The *Sue-Ya* has a modified deep-V bow, a 10-foot beam, and twin 160 engines. It's equipped with a Modar marine-band radio, a Bear Cat CB, a commercial graph-type sonar (Kelvin-Hughes) made in England for ocean use, Plath outriggers and downriggers, a Grizzly trolling indicator, and a hand-held Weller thermometer. Goodwillie uses rubber bands for releases and makes his own down weights, but sometimes runs Walker's Herbie. He uses Eagle Claw Powerlight 9-foot rods equipped with Penn 309 reels filled with 12-pound-test line on his starboard downriggers. At port he has an Eagle Claw Powerlight 8-foot rod equipped with an Ambassador 700 reel filled with 12-pound-test line and a Shakespeare Wonderod equipped with a Penn Peer 209 and 15-pound-test line. He uses Powerlights on the outriggers.

The water temperature at noon was 36 degrees in the top 10 feet of water when we started trolling north from the mouth of the Black. We put Hot'N Tots and Tiny Tads down at 6 feet. When Goodwillie turned toward shore, the temperature gauge I was holding rose to 38 degrees.

"A heat wave!" he said.

A spring salmon taken off South Haven, Michigan, at ice-out. Plath downrigger in background.

The Kelvin-Hughes showed fish being spooked by the boat, so Goodwillie put the outriggers down. At 1:00 p.m. we went in close to Deer Lick Creek in about 15 feet of water and got our first pop-up on the starboard outrigger flat line. "Fish on!" Goodwillie yelled. It bit a blue chrome Tiny Tad. At 2:30 we had our second strike over 20-foot depth. The fish, which had also taken the blue chrome Tiny Tad, got off before being played. At 2:45 we got a call from the *Sea Dog* saying they had hit two lakers on Hot'N Tots in 15 feet of water just offshore. "Those lake trout are climbing right up on the beach," Goodwillie said. There was a mud line in the current influence of the Deer Lick, and Goodwillie turned the boat to follow that. He put a chartreuse Loco and a Clown Spring Spoon dressed with Luhr Jensen reflector tape down, but the fish we were graphing ignored the offering. At 3:45 a coho hit the top of a double rig on the starboard downrigger. It was offering a Luhr Jensen Flutter Spoon. The down weight was set at 8 feet. The coho was about 2½ pounds. In the next hour we took a brown, a Chinook, and a steelhead. All five species. "A grand slam," Goodwillie called it.

The steelhead popped the Wonderod tip briskly and was out of the water before Goodwillie had the rod out of the holder. It leaped twice more and ran off 25 yards of line. The boat headed toward shore while Goodwillie played the fish and I took the wheel. "If we didn't have a net I

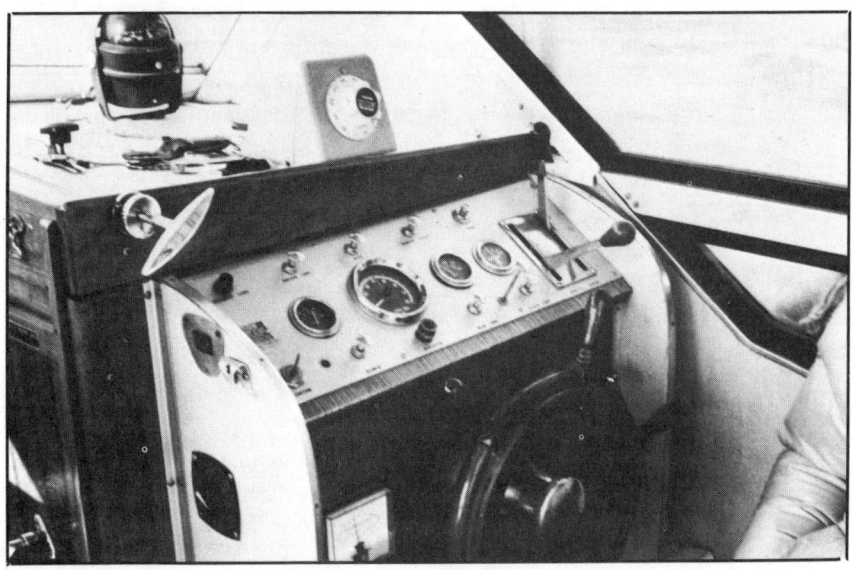

The control center of the Burgundy, showing wheel, compass, radio, and instruments, with automatic-pilot control at upper right.

could jump out and beach it," Goodwillie said. While I netted the fish the boat took another shoreward tack and Goodwillie dropped the rod to grab the wheel. The Jr. Flutter Devle hook caught in the net mesh, and the steelhead (about 3 pounds) threw it and flipped out of the net onto my foot.

That night the wind came up from the northwest, and when I joined Charter Captain Joe Kimmerly at the dock in St. Joe River, 25 miles south of South Haven, he said, "There'll be a little chop on the lake." I was wearing my down jacket and light wool trousers, and I had my long underwear and a raincoat in the stuff bag I carried on board. Captain Kimmerly and his son Glenn were repairing the chain drive on the automatic pilot in the cabin of the *Burgundy*, a 26-foot Marinette made by Aluminum Cruiser. Kimmerly, who has an interest in a factory in Niles, got his charter captain's license shortly after salmon were established in Lake Michigan. He's had many years' experience in boating on Lake Michigan. His son Glenn, charter captain of the *Brandywine*, is working his way through college by chartering during summers. He was on spring vacation from classes.

The *Burgundy* has a forefront, a sharp entry bow, a 10-foot–6-inch beam, and a Chrysler Marine 225-horse engine. It's equipped with a Regency marine-band radio, a Raytheon sonar graph, a hand-held Heath Thermo-Spotter M1-104 thermometer, and four hand-crank Riviera downriggers. The outside starboard and port downriggers have 18-inch arms and the inside stern downriggers have 6-inch arms. The *Burgundy* does not carry a CB. Kimmerly uses No. 16 rubber bands for releases and casts his own down weights. He uses Heddon Pal and Silver King rods equipped with Garcia Mitchell 301 and 406 reels.

After the automatic-pilot chain was repaired, Captain Glenn headed downriver for open water while Captain Joe and I went into town for sandwiches. We left the dock about an hour later, and as we headed into the Lake Michigan chop we got a call from the *Brandywine*. Son explained to father that he had taken four coho and lost one while trolling parallel to shore over 20-foot depth about a mile south of the river mouth. We started trolling toward the *Brandywine*.

The wind was stronger on the lake, and I put my raincoat on over my down jacket. The "little chop" Kimmerly had predicted became a violent up-and-down, and we chained the deck chairs to the gunwales. Although the waves were only about 3 feet, they were rough because we were running close in to the shore where we could see white froth breaking over the sand. I was making my second passage of the season and my stomach hung halfway between vomiting and adjustment to the motion.

The surface temperature, 42 degrees, was warmer than it had been at South Haven. "That northwest wind is carrying warm water to us from across the lake," Kimmerly explained. He shivered as he described the "warm" water.

At 10:45 we took our first coho on a silver-blue Tadpolly trolled 8 feet down over 20 feet of water. Kimmerly suggested that beer and a Dramamine might make me feel better. I thought that beer before lunch would make me dizzy, so we each ate a sandwich and a hard-boiled egg to prepare a foundation for the beer. The captain was right. My stomach felt better after the second beer. But my inner organs were chilled, so the captain surrendered the wheel inside the enclosed cabin and went to the stern to tend the downriggers. A down weight began to drag bottom, I didn't throttle down quickly enough, and the cable snapped, dropping the down weight into the lake. I felt clumsy, but the captain thought it was funny.

"I always lose a down weight on the first spring troll," he said.

At 11:30 we took a brown in the "honey hole" over 18-foot depth on a chartreuse-and-red Kush Spoon trolled at 10 feet. I pulled the automatic-pilot setting on and came out to net the fish, which was about 1½ pounds. A coho grabbed the same spoon as soon as it was put down, and Kimmerly netted it after I persuaded the fish to come to the boat. It was the same length as the brown. They were identically silver, but the brown had a football shape and black crosshatch marks. We made another pass over the honey hole, but there were no more taking fish.

At 3:00 p.m. thunderclouds had risen from the horizon line, and the wind had increased. All the waves now had definite whitecaps. The *Brandywine* called to say that they were going in. "It's too rough and windy to troll so close to shore," Captain Glenn said. We pulled our lines and headed for the river mouth. Kimmerly made coffee and I sat at the cabin table warming my hands on the cup. It was good to be under shelter. After we docked we sat at the cabin table playing cards, but the wind got worse, so we didn't go out again. We filleted the fish and had another pot of coffee. It was the end of the day.

During the night the wind stopped, and by morning it seemed warmer. I met Charter Captain Don Torba at the New Buffalo Charter docks in Oselka's Snug Harbor within the Galien River Harbor 30 miles south of South Haven at 7:00 a.m. The dawn light promised sunshine, and the lake was flat calm. Captain Torba was repairing a windshield wiper on his second charter boat, a 24-foot North American SS24, *NBC I*.

"Doesn't look like rain today," he said.

Torba, formerly a district sales manager for Holland Ranton, a drug company, started chartering in 1973 with a 20-foot Thompson. At that time he was the only charter captain in New Buffalo. Now there are five. There was one in Michigan City; now there are twenty. Torba, who's lived in nearby Three Oaks, Michigan, since he was eleven, founded the New Buffalo Charter Service, which was a loose affiliation of four cooperating captains. An experienced seaman, he often serves as transporting pilot for boats sold out of Florida factories. With a crew he brings them up the

Atlantic Coast and via the St. Lawrence Seaway into their new Great Lakes port.

Recently Torba bought a Skiffcraft, which will be briefly described in Chapter 14. The old *NBC I* still held in reserve in Torba's storage shed has a modified deep-V bow, an 8-foot beam, and a 235-horsepower inboard-outboard engine. It was equipped with a Modar 12-channel marine-band radio, a graph-type sonar Vexilar Model 155, a hand-held Fish Hawk combination depth counter and thermometer, a Grizzly trolling indicator, and Walker electric downriggers. The *NBC I* does not carry a CB. Torba uses both Walker releases and rubber bands. He uses round down weights with rudders that a friend casts for him. His North American was equipped with 9-foot Heddon Silver King rods set with Heddon 409A reels. The reels are no longer manufactured.

Four electric Walker downriggers are mounted in line on a plank across the stern of this 24-foot charter boat.

After the first mate, Bob McCormick, joined us, we cruised to a point off-shore from former Chicago Mayor Dick Daley's summer home where we started trolling at 8:00 a.m. over 50-foot depth. The surface water temperature was 41 degrees. McCormick spotted a fish on the graph at 20 feet. Torba set the down weights at 32, 13, 10, and 7 feet. "That 32-foot is a bit unrealistic, because the water's pretty cold down there," he said.

Ice-out in Lake Michigan

"Just in case there's an early-biting laker lurking there," McCormick said.

For insurance, Torba put a flat line out on the starboard side. It got an immediate hit, which we missed, then a steelhead grabbed a yellow Hot'N Tot on the line set at 7 feet. The fish, cold and sluggish, didn't jump; I was handling the rod and didn't know it was a steelhead until it was netted by Captain Torba.

McCormick reported a big fish mark at 46 feet, and Torba, who was putting the steelhead's Hot'N Tot back, down-ran it to that depth. He didn't have much hope of taking the fish. "But it's worth a try," he said.

The *NBC IV*, operated by Charter Captain Jim Hanson, came on the air to report that they'd taken four salmon over 40-foot depth in 7 to 10 feet of water. They bit Rappala Count Downs and Dardevle thin spoons. We trolled toward the *NBC IV* and took a coho on a Fire Plug at 10-foot depth with the line running 17 feet back of the down weight.

As we trolled past the *NBC IV*, Captain Hanson hailed us, saying, "Fish on! Big king!" We were in a little close and the line was heading our way, so we got all our down weights up and ran to a safe distance. I watched the action through my telephoto lens. It was a strange fight. The fish, after moving toward our boat, turned and chased the *NBC IV*. Usually they'll run a ways back, but this fish stayed with the boat. It jumped over a flat line that was still out, then ran under the boat, then dug deep. To prevent a tangle, Hanson cut the flat line the fish crossed. The rod was being handled by a customer, Larry Ellis, a private investigator from Lincoln, Illinois. His young son was on board and kept leaping up and down yelling, "Get him, Dad! Get him, Dad!" When the fish went deep and under the boat, Captain Hanson feared it would foul the line on the hull, so he goosed the throttle, and another customer, Mark Nelson, caught off balance, fell to the deck. After that Ellis was able to pump the fish up to the net. It weighed 12 pounds. I got a good boat-to-boat shot of Ellis waving his spring Chinook from the deck of the *NBC IV*.

This action occurred at noon, and we trolled along the shoreline without further bites until 1:55, when a fish hit a flat line and got off. At 2:30 we found a school of fish and took three coho in a row on lines trolled at 13, 14, and 17 feet over 45 feet of water. They were spring-sized coho—about 2 pounds, one perhaps 2½ or 3 pounds. The surface water temperature was still 41 degrees F., and at 10-foot and 20-foot depths it was the same. "Somewhere down there it'll be 40 degrees all the way to the bottom," Torba said. "We've just gone by spring turnover."

At 3:00 p.m. we took three more coho in a row, and that was it for the day. The *Beetle Bailey*, captained by Dick Gray, called in at 3:30 to say that their action had ceased. At 4:00 Hanson called to say, "It's all shut down over here." We went in with eight fish—a good spring day in marginal temperatures.

Much can be learned about outfitting a boat from this account of spring temperatures and spring fishing in lower Lake Michigan. The most important cross-comparison between these three seagoing captains is not that they all use rubber-band releases. (Torba used rubber bands intermittently and now has returned exclusively to Walker releases.) Probably the most basic cross-comparison is that all three carry downriggers, graph-type sonars (Torba now has a combination graph and flasher sonar), and thermometers. Harnessing these three into a working troika is the basic task of a downrigger captain. Another important factor is that all three boats are longer than 20 feet, have rough-water bows, and have beams of at least 8 feet. All of them have high freeboard and ample open deck space at the transom—the working place in front of the downriggers. All have marine-band radios—only one carries a CB. Although navigation is not difficult in early-spring offshore trolling, all three captains carry the NOA chart of their area on board at all times. All three captains coordinated water temperature, sonar readings, and down-weight depths to create productive trolling. All shared trolling information through radio message.

Only one captain uses a factory-produced down weight (Herbie), and that only part of the time. All of them use rods that are easily torqued to the down weight, pop up with good hook-setting strength, and forgive fish-fighting and boat-handling errors. Each carries a staggering number of lures to meet the multiplicity of a season's taking variables.

An atypical aspect of early-spring fishing is that the fish take at temperatures below the active ranges presented in Figures 5 and 6. The surface water temperatures were 38 degrees at South Haven, 42 degrees at St. Joseph (25 land miles south of South Haven), and 41 degrees at New Buffalo (50 land miles, but over deeper water), south of South Haven. This occurs because the fish are protein-hungry and cannot choose any other temperatures. The length of winter time a fish can fast varies greatly by individual metabolism from fish to fish. Moreover, some of these fish may be experiencing temperatures somewhat above the recorded surface temperature for at least a short time during the day. Another favorable aspect for the fisherman trolling among sluggish fish is that there are a large number of fish in the south end of the lake in early spring. Only a small percentage will take in sluggish temperature conditions, but even that small percentage can be a substantial number in a large population.

5
Hunting Fish with a Thermometer

In Chapter 4 we discussed the traditional way of fishing—by following the migrations. For most species, on most fishing banks there's a tradition of harvesting times built up from Indian lore, colonial experiences, commercial fishing, and a smattering of biological data. The fleet uses that data to follow and take fish. Today that's basically the way salmon are taken in the easily fished near-shore waters of the Pacific Slope. But when the salmon came to the Great Lakes there were no traditions. Furthermore, the salmon and the increased plantings of their trout and char cousins had to find their way through the Great Lakes in ways very different from their swimmings in their native waters. So the traditional ways were shattered on the shores of Lakes Michigan, Huron, Superior, and Erie at about the same time boats with homemade downriggers were wrecked on the beaches of Frankfort. A new method arose, called somewhat misleadingly, "temperature fishing."

All fishermen everywhere want to know where the fish are. They want to track them through the thousands of acres of water in lakes, impoundments, and oceans. A deer hunter uses tracks, spoor, and rubbings to figure out where the deer are concentrated. Fishing by following migrations patterns learned from Indians, colonists, biologists, and buddy-boats is a way of tracking fish. When the Great Lakes salmon disappeared shortly after being planted and everyone had to face the fact that there was no tradition for finding these new fish, a different

Downrigging at sunset off Oscada, Lake Huron. The captain at right is bowing in thanksgiving to the sun, which causes the thermal cycle that makes temperature fishing possible. (Courtesy Michigan Travel Commission.)

method of tracking had to be discovered. Fishing biologists in the Great Lakes racked their brains. Deer can be tracked because they have hooves, make manure, and rub trees when they're in heat. What do fish do that leave tracks in water? Biologists scurried to answer the question, because thousands of anglers afflicted with coho fever were clamoring for solid hook-ups with large fish.

Stan Lievense was assigned the task of teaching Michigan fishermen how to catch the newly planted salmon, the previously planted steelhead and browns, and the existing char. Many other biologists in other Great Lakes states joined with him, and he coordinated the gathering of fishing data from many research centers. Lievense, a graduate of the University of Michigan's School of Fisheries, served as a fisheries biologist for nearly twenty years in five of Michigan's Department of Natural Resources districts. For many years he was in charge of the Traverse City district, where he practiced good biology and good fishing. Although always aware of the most recent biological descriptions of fish behavior, he never forced the fish to follow their master's descriptions. Instead he met the fish with line and lure in the habitat they occupied. Thus he endeared himself to fishermen and biologists alike. He was often dispatched by the Lansing headquarters personnel to solve difficult fishing problems. He's the author of a pioneering temperature fishing pamphlet, "Catching

Great Lakes Salmon & Trout." Today he's the Michigan Travel Bureau biologist.

The downrigger was invented in the Great Lakes region at the same time Lievense began teaching the temperature method of tracking fish. Downrigger pioneers borrowed his knowledge; he built on their achievements. Because downriggers put the fishing lure consistently in the desired temperature habitat and troll it there, they test temperature theories. Thus Lievense became the father of temperature fishing in the Great Lakes.

Essentially, Lievense and other biologists had to find out what fish do that leaves tracks in the water. Fish move through water as the temperature of water changes. This is a fact of life for fish, just as leaving marks with their hooves is a fact of life for deer. But fish still do not leave tracks in the water with their fins. This shifts the emphasis from the fish's fins and skin (their temperature sensors) to the water itself. And here, Lievense developed a new analogy—a new way of explaining to fishermen. We find deer and bird habitat without leaving our cars by inspecting the trees. Birds don't leave many tracks, but we know that we'll find woodcock and grouse in aspens. And like aspens, water is a habitat. It's a temperature habitat. We can look for fish habitat from our boat, by checking water temperature. So the biological answer to our question shifts from tracks to habitat but is still rooted within the behavior of the animals we're chasing.

Thermotropism

Fish are thermotropic. This means that changes in temperature motivate their movement. Some fish will react to a change in water temperature of less than a degree. Usually fish's blood will be slightly warmer that the water they occupy. There are some warm-blooded fish that regulate their own body temperature instead of being dependent upon the water around them. The Atlantic bluefins for which we downrig off the Jersey coast are examples. But biologists say that most fish are cold-blooded animals that move away from areas of sudden temperature change. Each species has a preferred temperature tolerance range. The big word for this is "preferendum." The preferendum is the range of temperature (minimum to maximum) where a species chooses to be active and feed. The fish might move out of a comfortable temperature stratum where it had been resting to feed on another species in its nearby comfort zone. Lake trout, for example, resting in 41-degree water may move upward out of their preferred range to feed on alewife in 48-degree water.

But the lake trout wants to stay close to its preferred temperatures and will both rest and feed within that range if all of its needs can be satisfied.

I hope readers are adjusting to the fact that we must do something more complicated than track fish droppings through the water! We have to know more about the nature of fish than we have to know about the nature of deer. Before we discuss temperature in the life of the fish any further, we have to adjust to another shocking fact of life. We also have to know more about the nature of fish habitat than we have to know about the nature of deer habitat. Fish are thermotropic because of their nature and the nature of the water that surrounds them. And water changes temperature because of seasonal changes in the sun's energies, complicated by wind, waves, and many other variables. So this chapter must present a lot of water physics.

The major guidelines for easily understanding thermotropism and water physics are illustrated in the preferendum charts in Figures 5 and 6. See also Figures 9 and 23. Lievense created the salmon, trout, and char temperature range chart for use in the Great Lakes, the Pacific Ocean, and deep inland lakes that have lake trout. He also created the sports and forage fish temperature range chart for use across most of America. Norm Newman created the ocean fishing temperature chart (Figure 23) from his fishing experiences in the Keys, the Gulf of Mexico,

Salmon, Trout, and Char Temperature Ranges (°F.)				
		Preferred Temperature		
	Sluggish	Active Range		Sluggish
Steelhead		-10	58	+5
Brown trout				
Chinook		-10	53	+5
Coho				
Lake trout		-10	51	+5
	Subtract 10		Add 5	

Figure 5. *This chart is a handy memory aid for Great Lakes fishermen. Remember three numbers to establish the minimum and maximum temperatures for all the major sports fish in these waters. Subtract 10; add 5 to establish that lake trout, for example, prefer water habitat of 41 to 56 degrees F. Remember, Lievense cautions, that these are preferred temperatures.* When its preferred temperature is not available a species will seek habitat of the temperatures closest to preferred.

Pacific Ocean fishermen use this chart for finding habitat of two Pacific salmon (Chinook and coho) and one trout (steelhead). (Preferendum by Stan Lievense, Natural Resources Mgr., Michigan Travel Bureau. Printed with permission of the Michigan Travel Bureau.)

Hunting Fish with a Thermometer

and the Pacific. These charts are guidelines; they are not laws that fish must follow. Most of the fish most of the time stick to the stated preferred temperatures. But fish have reasons of their own for violating the guidelines. For a doctor the temperature of a patient is a normative guideline that can be taken and recorded daily and that gives an indication of what to look for within the body of the patient. Fishermen need to know enough biology and water physics to be able to make similar interpretations.

	Sports and Forage Fish Termperature Ranges (°F.)			
	Preferred Temperature			
	Sluggish	Active	Range	Sluggish
Largemouth bass	60	73	76	
Crappie	65	71	74	
Bluegill (large)	64	69	72	
Yellow perch	58	68	73	
Smallmouth bass	60	68	74	
Walleye	55	67	74	
Northern pike	55	66	74	
Muskellunge	55	63	72	
Brook trout	48	58	64	
Alewife	48	54	72	
Smelt	43	50	56	
Brown and rainbow trout	48	58	63	

Figure 6. *The minus-10, plus-5 rule used for the fish listed in Figure 5 won't work for these fish. Remember this chart is for finding the place in the water where the fish can exist. Sonar pinpoints the actual location. Lievense's rule applies for these species, namely: A fish species is most active at a given preferred temperature. When that's not available, the species will seek the temperature closest to it. (Preferendum by Stan Lievense. Printed with permission of the Michigan Travel Bureau.)*

From the point of view of the fish, their water habitat is composed of strata, pockets, zones of varying temperature. Each species has a preferred temperature range. It seeks the water strata and pockets where these temperatures exist. Fish wander (perhaps a few feet; perhaps several miles in a day), letting their skin, their biological thermometer, tell them which way the comfortable water lies. If each temperature stratum had water of a different color, the fisherman would soon learn that humpback salmon live in pink water, and he'd fish pink-water zones when he wanted to catch them. He'd be like a hunter seeking woodcock among quaking aspen. Unfortunately, water habitat is not so easily recognized as flora and fauna.

Tom Mandigo, who fishes and lectures with Mike Lummis, Walker's professional fisherman, doesn't always stick exactly to preferendum statistics. "It's not always practical," he says. "You can't find the temperature that fits." He uses his thermometer to identify sharp breaks in temperature—either up or down. He believes that temperature break is more important than biological preference in locating fish habitat. In a lecture to Erie Downriggers, Mandigo said: "We find that our springtime fish in Lake Michigan begin feeding at 37 degrees." This squares with my own observations when fishing in the spring of 1979 at Port Austin with Charter Captain Bruce DeShano, owner of the Off Shore Tackle Shop. We took lake trout in deep water near the lighthouse ranging in temperature from 37 degrees. Fishing shoreward in warmer water was not so productive. On the other hand, both of these examples are atypical. In spring the Lake Michigan fish have little choice—those who need to begin feeding to maintain metabolism must do it in very cold water. At Port Austin the lakers we were taking were probably early, spring-feeding members of a cold-water-preferring species. The charts give the best description of fish behavior when the fish have a range of temperature from which to chose. "The more mature a fish is the more he sticks to the preferendum," Lievense says.

So what the word "thermotropic" means and what fish actually do are often somewhat different. Usually a fish moves toward comfortable temperatures and away from uncomfortable temperatures. However, a fish running to spawn might remain in uncomfortable temperatures at the mouth of a stream and become sluggish. Some largemouth bass become so oriented to structure that they may not leave a favorite log even though temperatures go above their preferred 76-degree range. In this situation, they become sluggish. Fish will move out of oxygen-deprived waters into more oxygenated waters above their preferred range. Furthermore, each individual fish moves toward comfortable waters when his own internal thermometer is affected, and that may be somewhat above or somewhat below the statistical ranges for his species. In addition, ocean research data show that members of a species in one region may have slightly different temperature preferences from members of the same species in another region. Ocean data make it clear that species temperature preferences must be stated in fairly wide ranges—that we'll never find single optimum temperatures for fish-harvesting times. So, although we are discussing a tropism we say that differences in temperature *motivate* fish movement. We do not say that changing temperatures *determine* fish movement.

Hunting Fish with a Thermometer

Preferendum

I use the temperature preferendum to find fish habitat. Usually there are not enough animals to fill every existing niche in the woods. And there are seldom enough fish to fill up every acre of water that is their species' preferred temperature. So after finding the quaking aspen grove in the wetlands where worms live, we still have to send the dog in to find out whether woodcock are present. The dog on the boat is sonar. After and during our search for water of the correct temperature, we switch the graph on to inspect the water.

I don't expect fish to bite simply because I'm towing a lure behind a down weight through a school of fish in water at the midpoint of their active range. There's no magic temperature that ensures biting fish. Lures of the correct size, color, and aquatic wiggle still must be presented with skill. Temperature fishing methods put fishermen into contact with a pod of fish. Some of them will respond to the fisherman's degree of skills. Some will not!

Let's make a transition from fish to the intimate details of the water we're going to stick our thermometers into. Since bass, for example, usually live in a specific temperature range, we can find their habitat by probing with a thermometer. But we still need to narrow down the water we have to search by knowing what part of a lake will have temperatures bass prefer. We also need to know the season in which bass will find these temperatures. Limnology and oceanography give us partial answers to these questions. The most important limnological factor that helps us know where to use a thermometer is the seasonal, thermal stratification cycle. That cycle can be understood by thinking about dogs, sun, and shade. It's clear that as the sun moves, the shade moves, and the dogs move. In other words, the sun has a cycle and we know the places where shade occurs by that cycle. A body of water also has a cycle established by the sun, and downrigger captains know where to expect temperature habitat for the species they fish to in harmony with that cycle—seasonal, thermal stratification.

The Thermal Stratification Cycle

Because cycles don't really have beginnings or endings, they're hard to think about and to describe without oversimplifying. Fortunately most cycles have at least two meaningful poles. A twenty-four-hour day has noon and midnight as the positions of highest and lowest sun, and we can say that these are times of extremes—the sun is as high or as low as possi-

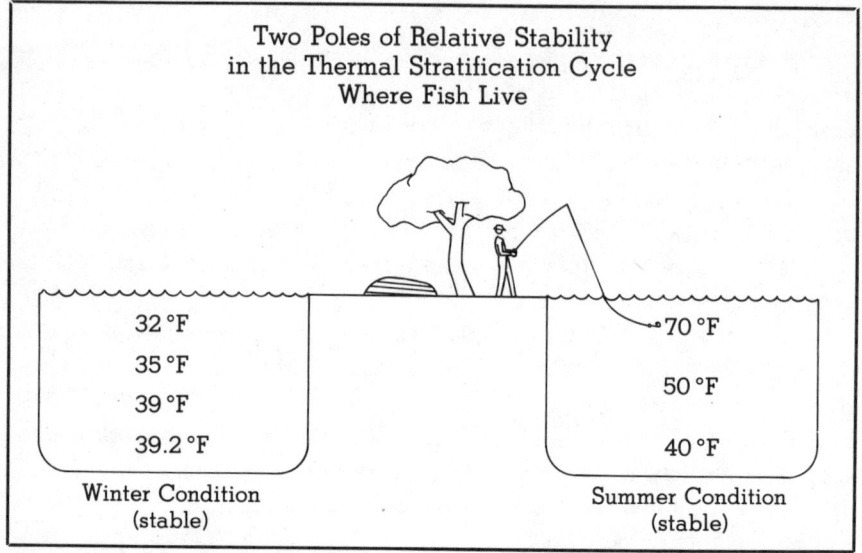

Figure 7. *This figure orients fishermen to the temperature habitat of fish. If these poles within the thermal cycle had been created for limnologists or oceanographers, we might have drawn them somewhat differently, perhaps to illustrate differences in thermal strata—three in summer, possibly two in winter. For us, the point is: What range of temperature habitat will the fish encounter during seasonal changes? The fisherman can remember these ranges by connecting three figures to the summer pole, four to the winter pole.*

ble. These facts help us organize our minds so we can talk to each other about daylight and dispatch trains. The same stability exists in the thermal cycle of most bodies of water. That cycle caused by seasonal sunlight and wind-wave action has two relatively stable poles. In his temperature fishing seminars, Lievense names them "winter condition" and "summer condition." (See Figure 7.)

In winter condition the surface temperature will be colder than 39.2. There may be a magic time when all the water is nearly the same temperature, so some authorities say that winter condition is isothermal. But Lievense believes that it's more helpful to fishermen to understand first that the surface will be colder than 39.2 and second that there's usually a descending order of warmth: 32, 35, 39, and 39.2. This is a relatively stable condition. It's stable because the winter sun has created maximum density. It's stable because ice protects large zones of water from mixing. During this time most fish will not feed, though ice fishermen may excite them into taking.

Summer condition is also a time of water stability. But the stability is not so great as in winter, because more variables are active. Summer stability is achieved by the creation of three thermal layers—epilimnion.

thermocline, and hypolimnion. In Figure 7, Lievense stresses three major temperatures (70, 50, and 40 degrees) rather than three thermal layers, because he wants fishermen to search for temperature habitat instead of searching for limnological phenomena. But it's important to understand this season as a pole of stability created by the resistance of the middle thermal layer to further wind-wave mixing of the sun's warming energies into the depth of a water body. This stability allows the creation of a major temperature habitat where fish can actively feed, grow, and take lures—the thermocline. Furthermore, as summer variables interact with each other, many minor thermal habitats are created in upper, middle, and lower waters where fish can actively feed, grow, and take lures.

We usually think this thermal cycle begins in spring when the sun's increasing warmth is transferred by wind, wave, and mixing currents to waters cooled during winter. This process is seasonal thermal stratification and seasonal thermal destratification. It occurs both in inland water bodies and oceans. However, in the ocean there is an additional force that creates thermal stratification—currents flowing from the arctic and subarctic. Some oceanographers call this stratification "permanent." Better terms are "main" or "semipermanent." In winter condition the 32-, 35-, and 39-degree water in Figure 7 is floating on the 39.2-degree water (water below 39.2 degrees floats; water above 39.2 degrees floats). The 39.2-degree water molecules are at their maximum density. That's why they are at the bottom. The cold water is where it should be—floating. The warmer water is where it should be—not floating. A wind will push the floating water ahead of it, over, and upon the dense water.

Step 1 in the cycle that creates temperature habitat is that spring sun warms floating water to maximum density (39.2), and these molecules, encouraged by wind/wave agitation, mix (step 2) into underlying water. For a time all a lake's water is the same density, and there's an exchange that may bring bottom waters to the top and vice versa—turn the lake water over. That's step 3. As the sun's energies continue warming the surface water above 40 degrees, it floats (step 4), and wind mixes it (step 5) into the colder underlying water. The mixing wind creates wave action, and the force of the wind/wave action creates a mixing underlying flow. That flow of sun-warmed water into colder water is not in the same direction as the wind. It often flows in an opposite direction. (See Figure 8.)

We've now discussed two ways fish habitat can be created—by sun warming, and by wind mixing. Every time the wind blows, a downrigger captain considers fish movement. The direction of the underlying current provides clues to places to probe with a thermometer.

The depth of water warmed by mixing will increase as spring proceeds

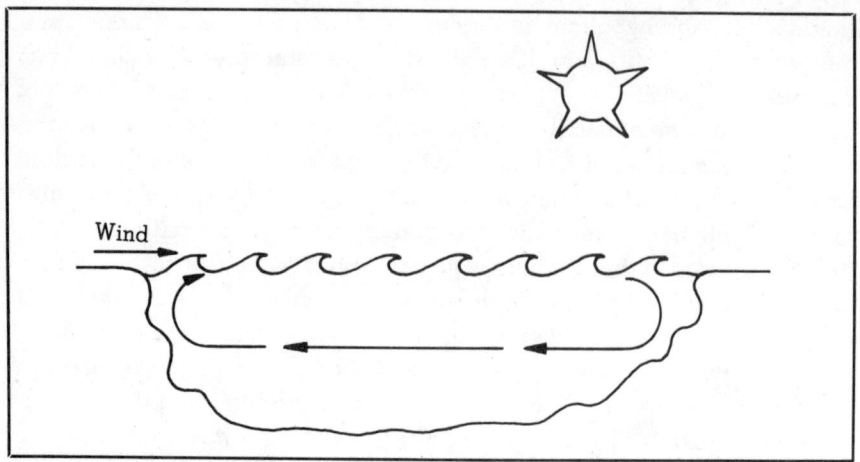

Figure 8. *Sun-warmed water mixing into colder water by wind-wave action. Fish will notice the underlying mixing current. Fishermen should notice that it flows opposite to wind direction.*

to summer and the sun's rays continue shining. In a shallow lake or pond the water will warm all the way to the bottom, but in a deep lake there will be several layers of temperature strata. As the upper layer continues to deepen, the colder, more dense water creates thermal resistance. Logically there would be a gradual progression from warm epilimnion to 40 degrees. If this could occur with stability, there'd be two layers in the thermal summer sandwich. Instead there is a zone of falling temperatures in a fast progression or in jumps. This zone is called the thermocline, which means "temperature slope." The Germans call it "jump-layer." The creation of the jump-layer is step 6 in the thermal stratification cycle. Step 7 is the summer stability created by the three-layer thermal stratification illustrated in Figure 9.

Of course, this is a dynamic kind of stability, because the thermocline layer may become deeper, hence the epilimnion thicker, or it may rise toward the surface, or it may be partially dissolved in one part of a lake by storms.

We now know three more places to check for fish habitat with our thermometer—the epilimnion, the thermocline, and the hypolimnion—and we've achieved roughly the same kind of cyclical knowledge of the patches of shade that a dog owner has when he looks for his dog in the shady side of the house in midsummer. Caution: It's popular to believe that the thermocline is the "ideal patch of shade" where all fish *always* congregate. It is not. It's true that for a few weeks each year the thermocline may become a narrow band of many temperatures providing a

Hunting Fish with a Thermometer

habitat for all Great Lakes species that is easily swept with down weights. But during most of the year, the preferred temperature habitat of the fish one seeks can be found in many places. And during all of the year the preferred temperature habitat can be found without knowing the depth of the bottom line of the thermocline. In fact, we can know all year long where the fish are without knowing exactly where the thermocline is. We are fishing for fish, not thermoclines. So use the thermometer to hunt fish habitat, not limnological events.

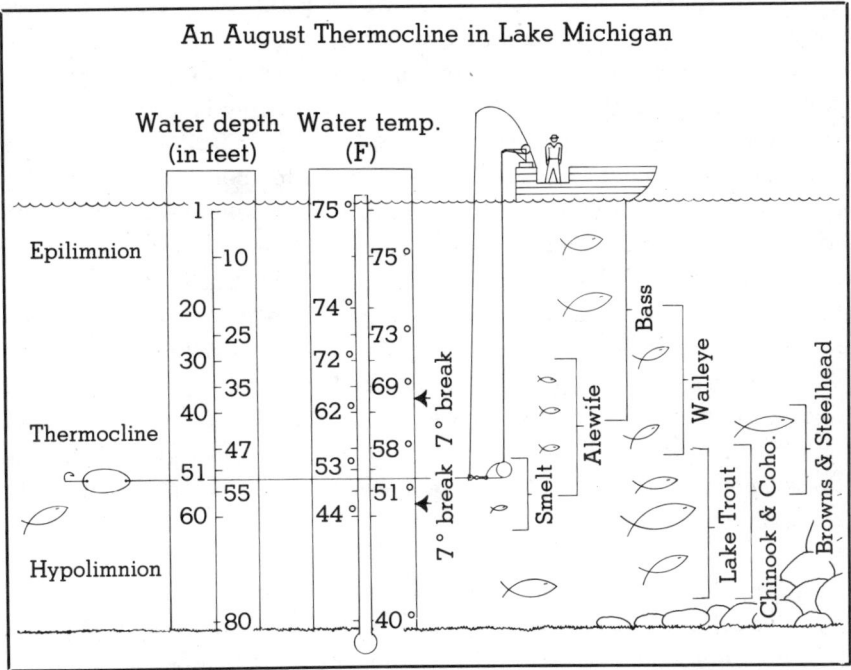

Figure 9. *Several species of fish are using the thermocline for habitat. It brings them and their forage fish together in a narrow, easily trolled band. There's structure for the species to relate to. This is an ideal thermocline with a 7-degree break at top and bottom. It looks more square and orderly in this rectangular figure than it really is. Notice that the thermometer that doesn't have mercury in it is an aid to thought. One fixed thermometer couldn't record all those temperatures.*

The Thermal Stratification Year

The new frame of reference we've learned, seasonal thermal stratification, will help us visualize taking places throughout the year in water bodies we fish. Let's go through a year on Lake Michigan.

During winter conditions the warmest place for the fish is in the 40-degree water, which could be at relatively shallow depths. The warmest place for the downrigger captain is in front of the fireplace. He may fantasize about putting caterpillar tracks on his boat and pulling a trench maker behind it to channel the ice for downriggers attached to the back of the trencher. Although all species will be sluggish, a very protein-hungry fish might take. After ice-out, as spring sun warms the waters, the downrigger captain will make his first temperature troll. If his harbor uses a stream inlet channel he'll check the stream temperature; then the temperature at 5-foot, 10-foot, and 15-foot depth from shore. He knows that his first trolling will be offshore and in stream inlets. When the wind blows toward his shore he'll anticipate a piling-up of warmed waters that will create more habitat and better trolling. The days will pass, the sun will warm more water, the winds and waves will actively mix upper waters, creating habitat farther offshore. The captain will go farther out, probing with his thermometer. He'll want to know the temperature over nearby shoals, and he'll begin to long for signs of a thermocline. He'll watch the wind, and if there are numerous bays in his area he'll want to know which bay is warmed first. Each time he goes out, he'll hail his buddies and ask them what readings they got at familiar underwater structures. As he hears weather forecasts, he'll anticipate the effect on the temperature habitats he's discovered. As spring changes to early summer, he'll become more and more concerned about relationships between depth and temperature. He'll possibly be fishing deeper water. He'll watch his thermometer for sharp changes in temperature. He's looking for the jump zone, the thermocline. He'll be hearing about the first thermocline from a buddy, or he'll discover one and tell a buddy.

By early June a well-defined second layer of water, which most limnologists would call a thermocline, will usually have formed over much of Lake Michigan. On the side of the lake toward which the wind blows, the captain may find very warm waters near surface, and the jump zone may be very near surface at that point. The captain will be excited about temperatures on his thermometer, which range 48, 46, 44, 42, and 41. He'll take lake trout in the first 33 feet either over shoals or over water of any depth. During June the captain may find 50-degree water at surface at the Michigan side and hear by radio from a buddy on the Wisconsin side that surface temperature is 55. On the Michigan shore the captain may find a 46-degree thermal line and, above that, readings of 51, 53, and 55. The 46-degree mark at, perhaps, 45 feet will be maximum trolling depth, and trollers may zigzag out for, perhaps, 5 miles. In August and September of 1942, captains found a narrow-band thermocline with temperatures providing habitat for all five species in temperatures of steadily colder progression. Here for two months they trolled productively in an ideal fisherman's thermocline! On August 22 on the Lake Michigan side about 5 miles out there was ideal water between 71-foot depth and 98-foot depth. Temperatures ranged 71.6, 64.4, 57.2, 53.6, and 46.4. This provided three different sets of 7.2-degree jump zones. Astonishing! The progression on the Wisconsin side of the lake was not so ideal. On September 13 and September 25, there was good thermal progression on both sides of the lake. On August 22 the water in the first 33 feet was too warm for salmonids except where the thermocline intruded upward at the Milwaukee shore. On September 13 most of the water above 33 feet was too warm for salmonid habitat. So for these two periods, structure, wind current, and upwelling within the first 33 feet could probably be ignored and the captain could have trolled only in the thermocline. But because this is ideal and because the captain was alert to the possible dissolution of the thermocline and the dispersion of fish by thunderstorms, he did not neglect point habitats. He was particularly alert to those gasoline-saving point habitats between his dock and the jump zone. He put his thermometer down and had his sonar running in each of these places as he went out with charters and watched the effect of changing winds upon them.

Captain Murrell Blackburn, writing in a *Great Lakes Steelheader* feature, "Troller Says Let Temperature Be Your Guide," says that as Lake Michigan summers progress wind is "the biggest determinant of the location of the thermocline." Offshore winds from the east push warmer water over greater depth, causing cold water to be pulled to the top along the shore and circulating warm water into the top of the deeper water. This may cause fish to move near shore because the water was cooled. Some may be disturbed by the change and head to more stable temperatures. Some may follow the wind direction into the thermocline being formed farther out to sea. "A south wind will usually move the thermocline deeper, but more slowly," Blackburn writes. "North winds will change the thermocline drastically, and quickly, depending upon the force of the wind. On a north wind, the fish usually scatter more. This is when you must search for the proper temperature farther out, in deeper, more stable water." From Blackburn's testimony it becomes clear that hunting the thermocline with a thermometer and adjusting trolling patterns to the dissolution and re-formation of thermoclines requires considerable detective work.

As the fall sun slants over Lake Michigan, the three layers dissipate; the lake moves from summer condition toward winter condition. At this time mature fish make spawning migrations to river mouths or, in the case of lake trout, to more shallow rocky bars. Because of these spawning mi-

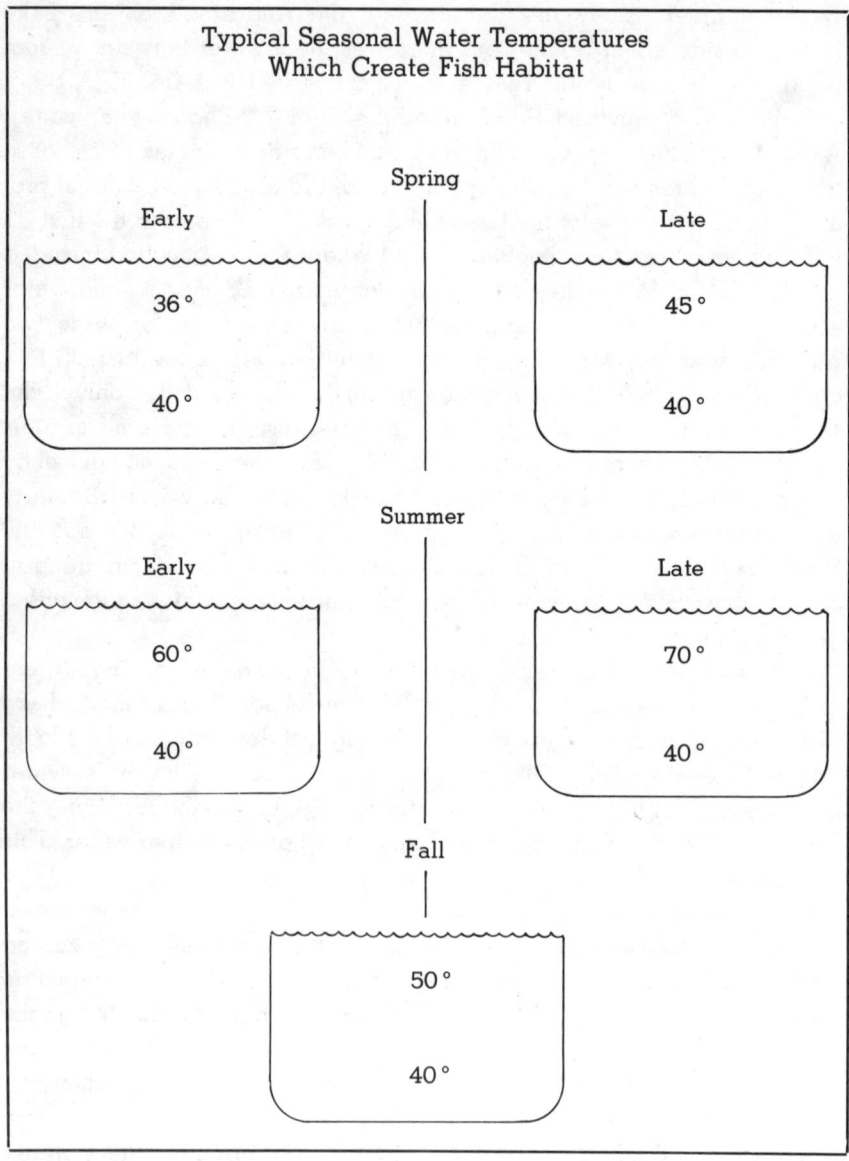

Figure 10. *This and the data in Figure 7 are counterpoint to the limnological thermal stratification cycle. To the fisherman, Figures 7 and 10 are foreground; thermal stratification is background. The limnologist may not see it that way, but the fish are likely to agree with the fisherman. Memorize these data or glance at them at the beginning of each season and use them as landmarks within your lake, where you may drop your thermometer to find thermal pockets, thermal bars, and breaks in temperature. (Data by Stan Lievense. Printed by permission of the Michigan Travel Bureau and the Michigan Department of Natural Resources.)*

grations, the captain trolls closer to the edges of the lake. Nevertheless, there may continue to be ideal temperature habitats in more central parts of the lake where sexually immature fish could concentrate. Finally the lake cools, winter condition sets in, the captain takes his boat out, and ice fishermen struggle with the habitat.

In this section we've covered a lot of data. A year is a long time, and years vary. How can the fisherman keep the thermal year in mind? Lievense (see Figure 10) has presented a simplified chart for a Great Lakes rule of thumb.

Point Habitats

Notice that as we've framed our water in terms of the overall temperature cycle, we've also included the migrations the fish make in accord with changes in water temperature. The next consideration is that point places or mini-habitats are created at sandbars, in bays, and over shoals where we can find fish. These habitats exist within the ongoing changes of seasonal thermal stratification. They are often more important to the troller because they occur just off his dock, around the corner and into the next bay, and between his dock and the thermocline out in the lake.

During the trolling season many captains run with surface thermometers on. Some have digital readouts for easy water reading. They are looking for thermal pockets—an area of colder water within an area of warm water. These may occur in bays, around points, at river mouths, and over deep bottom depressions. They may occur in surface water over a thermocline or in water so shallow that not all the thermal layers exist. In bays there may be a thermal pocket because one bay in the force of the prevailing wind is churned more than another bay. At points, currents change water temperature—one side is often warmer than the other. At river mouths inflowing waters may warm or cool the water mass. As downrigger captains move over the water, they attempt to anticipate the presence of thermal pockets by inspecting charts and logs, but only the thermometer can tell which water is cold and which is warm. So running with the thermometer on is important.

Ocean and Great Lakes upwelling causes temperature changes that attract fish. A good example is the West Coast from Point Conception, California, north to Cape Blanco, Oregon. There the prevailing northwest winds deflect surface waters offshore, causing vertical currents that bring cold waters from the bottom. This upwelling may cool surface temperatures by 5 to 10 degrees. Fish are attracted not only by the temperature change, but also by forage fish assembled to the nutrient-rich, upwelling bottom water.

Currents (which we know more about in the ocean) are another productive place for temperature hunting. A knowledge of ocean currents can appreciably contribute to downrigger productivity. An inspection of the current map in John G. Harvey's *Atmosphere and Ocean: Our Fluid Environments* shows that the Pacific Coast is influenced by the California Current and the Equatorial Counter Current. While fishing in the Pacific off the mouth of the Columbia River, I heard captains in Illwaco and Chinook discussing the "Japan Current." On some years it runs very close to the coast, they say. On other years the current is so far out that they must spend a night on the sea when fishing it. Captain DeShano has noticed much smaller currents created by wave action over rocky bars at Port Austin. These currents may run at right angles to wave action.

While fishing in the Pacific Ocean and Puget Sound I have seen a great many temperature places generally called rips, and sometimes called rip tides or slicks. A rip is a place of opposing forces. One side of the rip will be slick and calm; on the other side the water may be so turbulent that one will question whether it's safe to take a boat into it. The turbulence is not wave action. It's a series of agitated ripples and small whirlpools. One may see a flow of dirty water within the rip. There may be a lot of flotsam and ocean trash churning along the turbulent side. A rip can be pond-sized or as long as 15 miles. If one finds a rip after the turbulence has subsided, it may look entirely slick, like a lie for a gigantic Atlantic salmon. One side of a slick is usually cool, the other warm. "There may be up to 5 degrees difference in temperature from side to side," Mike Lummis reports.

Squawking, circling seabirds locate rips for fishermen. They are attracted by the baitfish that are disoriented in the water turbulence and temperature change. Some forage fish may be attracted by the temperature change, but some may be repelled. Sports fish come to the rips for the same reason the gulls assemble—to feed. Rips may not always be productive places to troll, becaue there may not be sports fish using the areas where the rips form.

Dick Seine, a commercial fisherman captaining the *Sonja* out of Illwaco, says that rips are formed by opposing currents. Joe Lesh agrees. Dave Davis says that Puget Sound rips may be formed by opposing currents flowing between the many narrow channels in that water body.

When trolling rips, remember that one species may like the warm side, another species the cold side. "Broadbill, swordfish and king mackerel will be in the cooler side of the rip," Norm Newman says. Dick Seine advises, "If you arrive when a rip is turbulent, run in the calm, dirty water, and let your downriggers work the turbulent water."

Hunting Fish with a Thermometer 41

Rivers may create thermal habitat. In early spring, shore water may be so cold that fish are sluggish. Sluggish brown trout swimming the Michigan shoreline, for example, enter the warmer water of the Cedar River in the Upper Peninsula and are warmed enough to start feeding.

How Wind Creates Point Habitats

Throughout this chapter we've discussed the importance of wind to water temperature. A few rules can be stated:
1. The wind may mix surface water with underlying water of different temperature. The surface may be cooled while the lower levels are warmed.
2. This process may stop if the wind dies without causing much temperature change or may go on to cause a complete turnover of temperature strata.
3. The wind may cross a landmass and push warm water away from a lee shore, allowing colder water to rise near the shore.
4. A wind may cross a sea, pushing warm water ahead of it into the weather shore, and a larger mass of warm water will pile up there. The prevailing westerly blowing from Illinois and Wisconsin across Lake Michigan serves to illustrate both rule 3 and rule 4.
5. A wind that sweeps over a large area of a body of water will have a greater effect on it than a wind that blows over only a small area. For example, a long lake on a north-south axis will be more affected by a north or south wind than by an east or west wind.

More Fish Behavior

Let's discuss two final aspects of fish behavior. After they've assembled in an area that satisfies their temperature range, each will seek out other aspects of the habitat that make them comfortable. Lake trout are more light-sensitive than other species. They want to be in cold water, but light will influence their choice between cold-water habitats. During early summer light the lakers are comfortable at 50 to 55 degrees; slightly above 100 feet. In the stronger light of late summer, they rest below 200 feet at 50 degrees. They'll probably move upward during times of slanting light to feed. Lake trout like to hug rocky bottoms, but can suspend. Coho orient to *near* surface; Chinook to *near* bottom. The two may be in the same temperature strata, but the Chinook may be closer to shore where they can be near bottom, the coho farther from shore where they can be near top. Brown trout will orient to structure and get tight against rocks and wrecks. Steelhead are cruisers. The like to be alongside the bottom area where they can move—perhaps along a bar or at the tip of a point, or in river-mouth current. Habitat of the correct temperature should also have other characteristics a species likes. If a temperature stratum covers a large area, as thermoclines sometimes do, the various species will disperse through it to the cover they like. After downrigger captains find temperature strata with thermometers, they may search further with sonar for structure and fish.

Be aware that fish have the ability to rest and feed wherever they find comfortable temperature. They need not have their "feet on the ground." They can get along without structure and suspend. In water, a fish is nearly weightless. It can expand or contract its air bladder to compensate for the different pressure at different depths. Fish must remain upright so they can work their gills correctly. That's called maintaining station. But they can do this at any depth. So fish can rest in any water that doesn't sweep them away or tumble them. A fish may prefer to lie against a bottom rock when resting, but it requires no more effort for it to suspend in comfortable temperature 15 feet below the surface over 200 feet of water. Nevertheless, shoal fish (salmon, trout, and char) will choose the part of a temperature habitat that has structure they like over the part that has no structure.

Summary

The theme of this chapter is not that fish bite at a certain temperature. They are more likely to bite within preferendum minimums and maximums, but that doesn't mean that we use thermometers to guarantee the fish will bite. The theme is that we can find fish habitat with a thermometer. From a boat most water looks like good fish habitat. From a car window most trees look like good woodcock habitat, but aspen groves in low, wet places are better habitat than oak groves on high hills. Just as we look for woodcock where certain trees tell us there are good worming places, so we look for fish in water of temperatures where forage fish could be eaten. After we find the temperature habitat for the species we seek—for example, 43 to 58 degrees for Chinook and coho—we turn on our sonar to see whether there are fish present. In the same way, we turn the dog out to check an aspen grove to see whether woodcock are present. Fish do not use all of the water habitat of correct temperature. Predators may have driven them out, or there may not be correct structure to which they can orient, or the right temperature may have been achieved by the wrong water forces. In the Columbia River, for example, high discharge of cold rainwater might be accompanied by excessive silting, which drove fish out; or a combination of tidal and river forces

Hunting Fish with a Thermometer

that irritate fish might have occurred. If the right temperature is achieved by water forces that bring food for forage fish, the chances of fish being present may be increased. Upwelling off the coast of Oregon may come at a time when salmon were about to be driven off by increasing warming from summer sun and winds from the south. This upwelling, which cools the water, also raises ocean nutrients that attract forage fish, and salmon remain to feed on them. Here two factors are operating to attract fish, and both are related to temperature changes.

Still, those who hope to transform temperature fishing into the surefire thing will ask: "Isn't that preferred temperature on the charts the magic point where the fish are supposed to bite?" The answer is: "Yes, that's the magic point for the magic fish." But there's no such thing as a magic, or ideal, fish! Each fish has its own personal preferendum. Furthermore, the preferendums of fish probably vary widely from geographic region to region. Each captain should keep a diary and, by averaging, develop a preferred temperature for his own port.

Thermometers help us locate fish habitat. Sonar helps us locate fish within habitat. Skilled presentation of lures of the correct size, color, and aquatic wiggle helps us take fish.

Thermometers

Don't try to check water temperatures by lowering a kitchen thermometer. If the thermometer is lowered through more than one temperature

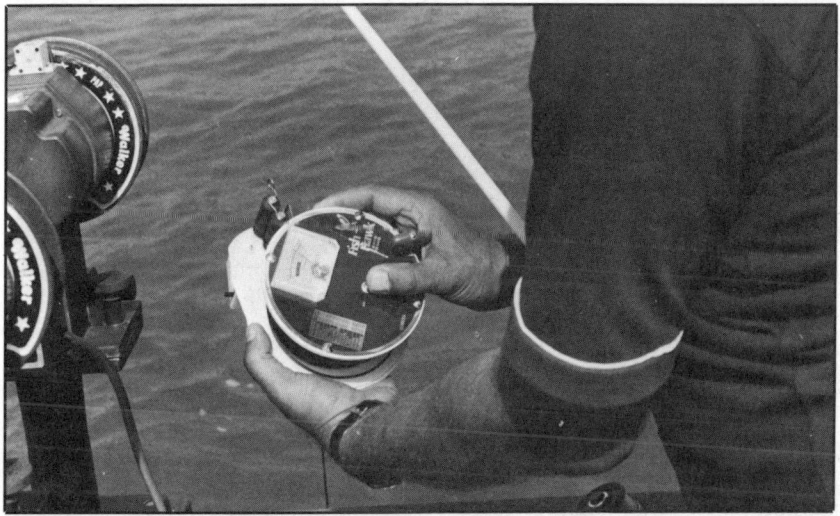

A Fish Hawk combination temperature and depth gauge. Right thumb is on temperature switch. Note the cord rollers above the temperature gauge.

level it will give an accurate reading only for the last level through which it passes on retrieve. An electronic cord should link the thermistor and the temperature gauge. The captain is checking for both depth and temperature, because he wants to coordinate the depth of troll with the desired temperature. So the kind of depth–read-out device on the thermometer is of particular importance.

Downriggers can buy surface and deep-probing thermometers. There are three deep-probing types—hand-held; downrigged sensors with a cord that carries the electronic information to a digital read-out; and downrigged cordless. Surface thermometers have a through-the-hull sensor attached to an instrument-panel dial. They satisfy the captain's desire to keep in touch with the water under his hull at all times, because they read the water at running speeds. In early spring and late fall when running near shore, surface temperature may tell the full story. At other times of the year, sharp breaks in surface temperature are places where the captain will want to lower the sensor, usually called a thermistor. The hand-held thermometers lower a weighted thermistor from a cord storage device held in the captain's hand. They also have read-out dials. The cord can usually be cranked back onto a revolving spool. On some models the cord is retrieved by hand winding onto a dumbbell-shaped storage spool. Depth is coordinated with temperature on most hand-held models by inspection of color coding on the cord that transmits from the thermistor to the read-out dial. The disadvantage of hand-held thermometers is that readings must be obtained while the boat is motionless. If the boat is under power or being pushed by wind and waves, the cord planes out and the depth at which temperatures are obtained is uncertain. Downrigged thermistors will read out temperatures at reasonably exact depths, because the down weight holds the cord at accurate right angles to the surface.

Current from a thermistor can be sent through a wire braided into a downrigger cable. But it takes a special wire, so incorporating a thermometer into a downrigger has proved to be a difficult task for manufacturers. Hand-held thermometers can be separately rigged to the down weight, and the conducting wire is reeled or rolled as the weight is raised or lowered. But this has disadvantages. There's an extra line in the water, and it may not take trolling speed as well as a cable. The thermistor is usually attached to the place where a fish line would be attached, so that downrigger isn't fishing while temperatures are being studied. A thermometer that continuously "reads" temperature where the down weight is trolling is a highly desirable tool.

In addition to surface thermometers with cockpit dials, Lowrance sells

Hunting Fish with a Thermometer

a hand-held thermometer. The electronic cord indicates depth by color code, and it's stored by hand winding onto a dumbbell-shaped spool. Both the Heath Company Thermo-Spotter Model No. M1-104 and the Mac-Jac Model 600 hand-held thermometers give depth by color-coded cables that crank onto revolving spools. The Waller Company Fish Hawk temperature digital depth counter gives the depth of the thermistor on a counter similar to downrigger counters. It's mounted beside the temperature gauge on the compact, hand-held revolving spool that stores the cable. As far as I know, it's the only hand-held deep-probing gauge that has a depth counter.

Riviera's Temptroll combines a thermometer and a downrigger. This is a trolling unit with a special electronic cord woven into the down cable. It comes with the read-out gauge on the unit or remotely mounted. When the down cable breaks, the electronic cable also breaks. With Temptroll the captain has a continuous temperature reading for the lures he's trolling behind that particular down weight. He need not stop to obtain temperature data. He's always in touch with the underwater habitat within his trolling depth. He knows the temperature of the habitat of fish he sees with his sonar. These are important advantages that increase the captain's ability to coordinate fishing variables. Jim Rieth, Riviera president, says that development of Temptroll has caused many headaches, but it's working well. Luhr Jensen once produced a combination downrigger and thermometer called the Auto Temp. They've been discontinued, but many are still in use, and they're valued like older-model Thunderbirds. Jack King in Muskegon, Michigan, still maintains them.

Bill Sherwood, president of the Waller Company, makers of Fish Hawk, reports that his executives are designing a cordless thermometer that can be sent down on any downrigger. The device will by telemetry application "radio" temperatures to an on-deck gauge.

All thermistors should be checked for error with a mercury thermometer. Some have a consistent error for which the operator must adjust.

6
How to Use Sonar Graphs and Flashers

"Sonar T" is my phrase for sonar's adaptation to downrigger fishing. The word "sonar" is a marriage of the words "sounding," "navigation," and "ranging." These words describe sonar's navigation usage. Now it's become the eyes of the captain who's watching his down weight and searching for both fish and fish habitat. So sonar has become a trolling tool. "Sonar T" stands for "sonar trolling."

Originally sonar was developed to deal with the troublesome problems of working a boat. Captains need to know the depth under their hulls not only because of the continuing possibility of collision with shallow-lying and floating objects, but also because searching for the safe depth between reefs and through channels is a time-consuming worry. (They also need to know the kind of bottom when anchoring.) They need this information continuously, like a blind man tapping his cane, and sonar, which works day and night in clear weather or fog provides it without coiling ropes, casting lead, or yelling marks.

The trolling captain also has navigation problems. Added to this, he desires to see the fish's underwater world. Are there any fish there? Are they in catchable number? What is their depth? What kind of structure are fish using? These are questions that go beyond sonar into sonar T.

A sonar sends sound to receive echoes. Electronic apparatus translates the echoes into symbols that tell depth, configuration of underwater objects, and the hardness of the objects from which the signals echo.

How to Use Sonar Graphs and Flashers

Michigan Department of Natural Resources officer uses a Lowrance LRG 1510B graph sonar to locate nets illegally set by poachers in Lake Huron. The round device to left of graph is a Brinkman spotlight. (Courtesy Lowrance Electronics.)

Depth is easily obtained. It's a measurement of the time it took for a sound to go forth and come back, and it's easily read out on a chart calibrated in feet.

The sending of electronic signals to receive echoes also gives two other kinds of information. Measurement of the amount of the sent signal that's absorbed into the echoing object gives us one kind of information. The configuration of a continued receiving of echoed sounds gives us another kind of information. If the response of a signal that echoed from an absorbing object is weak, it will make a weak light on a receiver. Mud absorbs electronic signals, so a weak signal can be interpreted to mean "mud bottom." It might also be muck or a combination of muck and mud. If the echoed response is strong, then not much of the sent signal was absorbed by the echoing object. Hard rock bottoms return strong echoes; gravel bottoms return less vigorously, but with more rebound than mud. The shape of the object against which the signal echoes creates a distinct light or stylus pattern. That pattern is painted in silhouette on a graph-type sonar receiver and in light rectangles on a flasher-type receiver. So we get three kinds of information from sending and receiving sound.

Two types of sonar take their name from the kinds of receiving dials or screen—flasher and graph. Interpreting the signals on these screens requires practice. Neon bulbs on flasher dials paint light or lighted rectangles. Some people call these rectangles dashes. Some of the rectangles are wide, some narrow, some bright, some weak. From them a captain can tell what his depth is, what kind of bottom he's over, and whether large and small fish are present. A stylus on a graph screen inks received signals into drawn configuration. These are usually more easily read by laymen than lighted rectangles, because the stylus-drawn shape of a tree looks more like a tree than a skinny rectangle.

The graph symbols have another advantage. They are permanently inked onto paper and can be read after returning to the wheel from tending fishing lines. You have to watch a flashing light every second to see its symbols. Many people call all sonar devices "graphs." The word has overwhelmed the words "flasher" and "sonar." However, correct usage is "graph-type sonar" and "flasher-type sonar."

Graphs are favored by Big Water trollers because they operate fairly large boats and spring around the deck tending lines and landing fish. Flashers are used by bass fishermen or others who may be operating smaller boats in fairly shallow water. The bass fisherman can often watch a flasher, run his engine, and fish from one position. He can keep one eye on the flasher light, which paints and moves on. On larger boats in Big Water, captains need the more permanent record provided by graph paper. After tending a line or netting a fish at the transom, one can return to the graph and read the record of the bottom configuration and the fish above it.

Some captains like to have both. Graph paper costs money, and, if you run a lot, it's cheaper to run the flasher when you're coming into port or going out to sea. Then your only need may be for avoiding collision, and you don't need a complete readout of habitat and fish. Another reason for having both is that on long boats graphs mounted to monitor the stern may not give early enough warning of floating objects under the bow.

All sonar is based on the fact that sound travels through fresh water at the speed of about 4,920 feet per second. Sound travels faster in water (it isn't absorbed, as light waves are) than in atmosphere. Because sound travels faster than a boat, it's all right to run with a sonar device operating. There may be some distortion and interference as you run, but that can be adjusted with the knobs on your set and does not come from your relatively slow speed. Searching for fish as well as searching for hazards to navigation while running is all right. As Nick Venditti, Lowrance fishing professional and zone sales manager, is fond of saying, "My bass boat cannot outrun the speed of sound."

A sonar, both graph and flasher types, has two major assemblies—the

How to Use Sonar Graphs and Flashers

head and the transducer. The two are connected by a flexible cable. (Never cut it!) When the power is on, the head sends an electrical impulse to the transducer. That impulse activates a crystal that generates a high-frequency sound signal. On return echo, the signal is received by the transducer, changed into another electrical impulse, and transmitted to the head, where it's reported on graph paper or a flashing dial.

Technicians think of the head as a carrier or electronic power pack that sends pulses of energy. These pulses are short and of high frequency. They return to the transducer from underwater objects in a weakened form, and they're amplified en route to the neon bulb or stylus that records the appropriate symbol. As the echo's signal is recorded, another sound signal is sent out. This happens so incredibly fast (the sound pulsations are expressed as milliseconds) that a large rock or fish can be fully painted by the light or stylus in an instant. Each recorded fish represents many received echoes—a representative sounding rate for a flasher sonar is about twenty-four times per second.

It may be difficult for you to understand your transducer. It does two conversions, and it sends in two directions. The double arrow in Figure 11 will help you. This arrow should correct your natural feeling that there's a radio station transmitter somewhere that sends for you when you turn on your sonar set. You and your set are sending. Furthermore, you

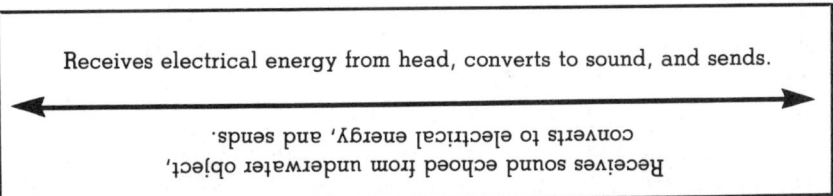

Figure 11.

are sending two kinds of pulsations—first, electrical pulsations (watts) from the sonar head to the transducer; second, sound pulsations from the transducer to underwater objects. Moreover, you and your set are receiving. The transducer eye receives echoed sound and sends converted electrical energy to the head, where it's painted for you on a graph or flasher screen. Read the sentences above and below the double arrow.

The transducer has not done its job until it has done two complete transformations of energy. Furthermore, the transducer is both the transmitting and the receiving antenna of a sonar.

We are now ready to define echo transducers. They convert energy of one kind into energy of another kind and stand by to reverse the conversion. They are electroacoustic transducers.

If you want to be sharp about shopping for sonar sets, you may want to know more. There are two types of transducers—magnetostrictive and ceramic. Magnetostrictive transducers can take almost unlimited power and can usually be overloaded without damage. There's a further advantage. Low-frequency sounders usually give a wider beam angle to observe a larger area beneath the boat. Magnetostrictive transducers are used with higher power–low-frequency sets because they forgive overloading and cost less than the second type, ceramic transducers. Ceramic transducers have a higher efficiency factor, but the lower the frequency the higher the cost, and they can be damaged by receiving higher power. The technicians who built the set you buy may have already discounted for problems you anticipate with your new knowledge. So apply your wisdom with respect for clearly stated guarantees.

The sound pulsations spread out from the transducer to sweep a specific section of the bottom. This is expressed by the confusing term "cone angle." The term is helpful because it tells us that the effective sending range of a sonar is cone-shaped. The term hinders thinking because we get the impression that the bottom end of the cone is flat. It isn't. It's convex. Figure 12 shows the correct sending shape (acorn) of pulsations from a transducer. This figure also shows that the pulsations extend closer to the bottom at point A than points B and C.

The acorn-shaped pattern wells outward. Obviously the signals sent horizontally into the water are dissipated and do not echo back effectively. The effective echoing occurs between the transducer eye and the bottom. At bottom where fish may be hugging structure, some of these echoes are weak, and most of them are obscured in the black carbon the stylus on a graph paints to show bottom. Many bottom-hugging fish are not seen on the flasher or graph. Some manufacturers correct *most* of this error by using a white line, by adjusting the sensitivity of the set, or by using several scales. Nevertheless, be prepared for takes from bottom-hugging fish that you and your sonar don't "see," and work with the down weights for these "invisible" fish.

Sonar sets vary in their effective angle, that is, in the amount of the bottom they sweep or scan. The downrigger fisherman probably needs a set that has an effective scanning cone of 22 degrees. He may need somewhat more; he's not likely to be happy with less. There's a maximum size of scan that should be considered. Any cone so large that it's difficult to tell where the fish are may be too large. So spending money for a set that scans a wide path may be wasted effort. This is a technical question that buyers should discuss with representatives from several manufacturers. When seeking a wide cone, be certain that power from the head increases

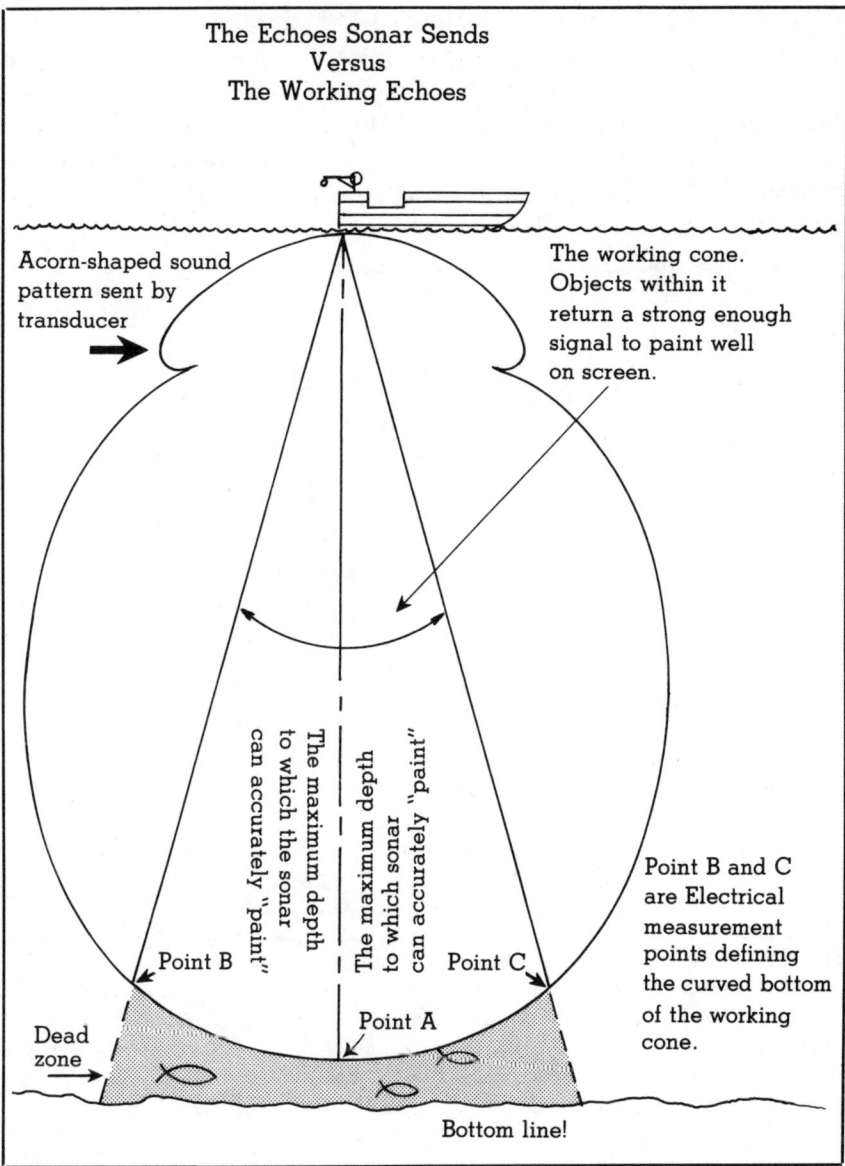

Figure 12.

enough to give clean readings. Notice from looking at the figures that width of cone scan increases with depth. "Finally, when shopping for cone angle be certain that you compare apples with apples," Skip Christman, Vexilar electronics technician, cautions. The norm for measuring a cone angle is to measure the effective width of the cone at 3 decibels on a test pattern. (See Figure 13.) In this figure the fan-shaped grid represents measurements of decibels of sound sent in the acorn shape from the transducer eye (black circle). An effective cone angle has been drawn on the fan-shaped grid. Most manufacturers measure the width of their cone along the 3-decibel arc. However, it's legal to measure it along a lower arc. Although this would make the cone angle larger, the set would not be more effective.

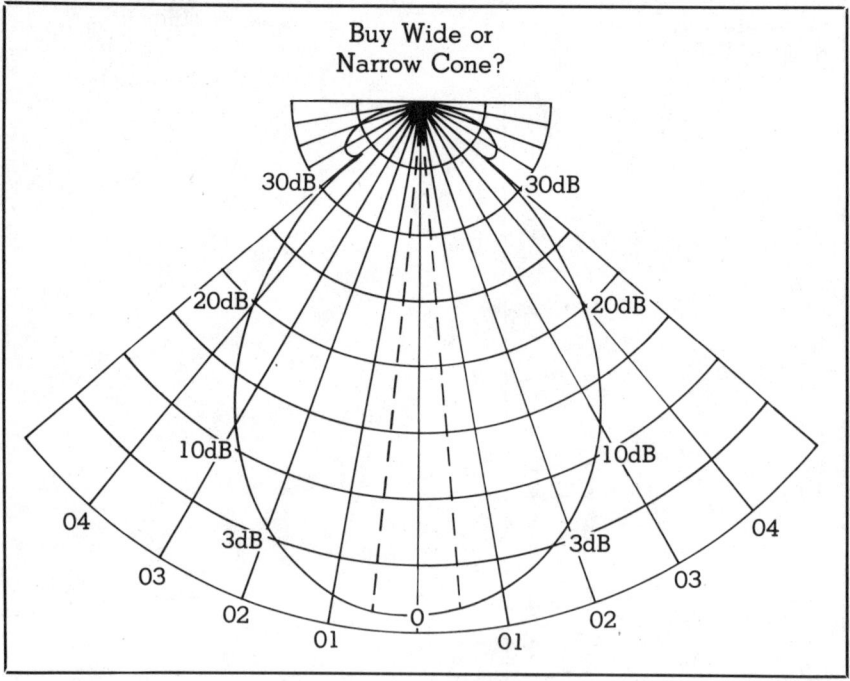

Figure 13. *This shows the actual acorn pattern a transducer made when tested on a machine that shows a decibel grid. The line below 4 dB is not 2 dB; 2 dB is four squares below 3 dB. If you're comparing a set that advertises a wide cone with a set that advertises a narrower cone, be sure both were measured at the same decibel point. Advertiser B can tell the buyer that his sonar sweeps with a wider cone than that of Advertiser A if he lowers the measuring point. But at that point, the power may be so weak that not all of the echo returns.*

The most important thing in using sonar is to read the dial of your unit correctly. Most fishermen get enough information from their sonar to improve their fishing. But reading what a sonar paints is more difficult than reading an x-ray. When a doctor reads an x-ray he knows what position the patient was in when the picture was taken. And there are standard positions that the x-ray technician will have the patient assume. With sonar shot from a boat bouncing on the waves and approaching the target

How to Use Sonar Graphs and Flashers 53

blindly, the angle of the "camera" will vary widely from shot to shot. You seldom see a sunken boat from the same angle; wind, wave, and blind reckoning create a new picture on each pass. The fish your transducer eye is "seeing" is awash in a volume of water, and it can turn 360 degrees on many radii. The transducer may "shoot" the fish from any angle. The angles of tilt from the wave-lifted boat are less variable for fixed structure or for bottom. For these reasons it's very difficult to set up a way of teaching the fisherman how to read his graph or flasher. The Lowrance firm has done an excellent job of presenting the major images a fisherman may see on graph and flasher. *The New Guide to the Fun of Electronic Fishing*, published by Lowrance, has basic drawings of graph readings. Skip Christman, in *Seeing Your Underwater World*, has presented many pictures that help fishermen learn how to read graphs and flashers. The Si-Tex Company is producing pictures that students of sonar can study. But the difficulty is that graphs and flashers are not TV screens replaying shots taken by an underwater photographer. They are underwater x-rays taken from all kinds of angles. The viewer must do some interpreting.

Christman says that he gets sets from people who want them repaired so they'll show pictures like the ones in the instruction manual. "It's a headache," he says. "I have to explain that there's nothing wrong with the set." He urges that people practice over a known underwater area. "Go out and sink a milk can full of cement," he says. "Then go over it with your unit from north to south. Then cross the can from south to north. Observe the difference in the 'picture' you see." He goes on to urge that the milk can be approached and studied on a day of high waves and a calm day. Then find a reef with a drop-off, a lake with trees, a lake with a grassy bottom. In all cases be certain you can find these underwater objects again. If you're using a graph, keep the graph paper on file by date and water conditions. Thus you can build up a library of "x-rays" to study. When you're out with your unit and you find a puzzling underwater object, grapple for it with a lure or hooks you've prepared ahead of time. "A sonar is not a magic box which presents a TV image of fish and habitat," Christman says. "It's an instrument requiring interpretive experience."

A graph "picture" strips away all the water as an x-ray strips away all the flesh. This can give you a static distortion and cause you to look for easily recognized objects like fish, or your jigged lure, or your down weight. Do not be easily satisfied by your recognition of familiar objects. Instead, look at each mark the graph makes. What is that black smear? Keep asking. It's something painted by your machinery's reaction to a bounced echo. What could it have bounced off of? Why did it paint in that shape? Try to make another pass over the object with the gain set differently. Force yourself to interrupt fishing to do this. Did the object make an echo mark? If so, what would be a correct gain setting for getting a good shot of this object?

I said that sonar strips away all the water. Not quite all. Dense water will return some echoes, so a thermocline that has dense water will sometimes show on a graph.

"Using sonar to find fish started in 1957 at Joplin, Missouri, with the Carl Lowrance family," says Thayne Smith, Lowrance Electronics public relations director. Carl Lowrance fished for bass, and his sons Darrell and Arlen were among the first inland skin divers. Naturally the father sent his sons underwater to see what the fish were doing. From their reports it became clear that large water areas have no fish in them, that fish school together in areas where they're comfortable, and that these areas change with season and temperature. The Lowrances realized that an instrument was needed to give fishermen underwater sight. There's no point in fishing water where there's no fish, and although there may be many areas where fish can be comfortable and find forage, not all of these areas are used. Darrell Lowrance interrupted his study of electronics at the University of Arkansas to help his family develop instruments to give fishermen underwater sight.

We'll be better able to interpret the new symbols we've been studying if we know more about their creation and the sources of error in their creation. For fish, graph-type sonars paint a "symbol" usually referred to as a U, a V, a hyperbola, or a "fingernail shape." "Look at all those fingernails," Captain Torba is fond of saying. There's a reason fish usually have a fingernail shape. Let's imagine a transducer angle of 40 degrees at a depth of 15 feet. As a large fish enters the leading edge of the cone, it's below and about 32 feet ahead of the transducer. As the boat carries the transducer over the fish, the distance from it to the fish decreases to 25 feet—the real depth at which the fish is swimming. As the distance from fish to transducer lessens, the marks on the paper rise. The transducer continues forward, the distance increases, and the graph marks move down on the paper. An upward-swimming fish paints a more vertical mark on graph paper. A still fish under a drifting boat will paint a longer symbol. A downward-moving fish will paint a wide U.

Fish having the same recorded shape, at the same depth, and on the same graph paper can be seen as larger or smaller than one another. Within that perspective, size can be interpreted. But remember that as depth of fish increases from, say 20 to 60 feet, a larger symbol may not mean a fish larger than one painted at 20 feet. The larger symbol at the

How to Use Sonar Graphs and Flashers

greater depth may have occurred because it took the transducer longer to pass over it. Remember there's a wider cone scanning the deeper fish.

Other distortions occur from the way the transducer "sees." These should be kept in mind as you read the symbols on your graph or flasher. In Figure 12 there are fish under the arc BAC that might not show. They might be out of effective range; they might be obliterated in the ink the stylus uses to paint the bottom.

There are problems in discriminating and reporting objects both at the surface and at the bottom. White lines are used on graphs by many manufacturers to solve this problem. In addition, Vexilar has a Sea Bed Discriminator on some models, and Lowrance has a patented gray line on many models. The white line is created by sophisticated circuitry that allows a unit to separate the surface and the bottom with a fine, black line and a white band. At the surface, debris and plankton are separated from fish; at the bottom, rocks and other objects are separated from fish

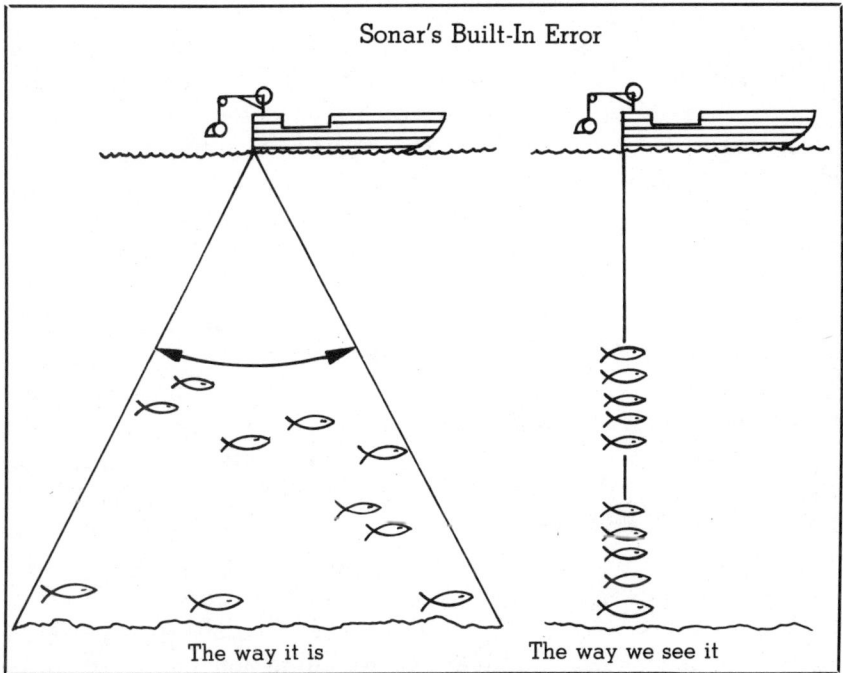

Figure 14. *Error 1:* The fish are aligned with side-to-side compression so they seem to be neatly stacked one above the other. If you're watching the graph or flasher as the boat runs, some of this error will be apparent as the fish are picked up one by one, but if you return to the sonar by the wheel after adjusting a downrigger, you may not see the fish in correct relationship. *Error 2:* Fish that are at the same depth from the sonar (they may be widely separated) paint as one fish. For clues, watch for fuzzy overlaps as the graph paints.

and bottom cone-angle errors are corrected. At both surface and bottom, stylus inking on graphs that hides objects is cleaned up. Lowrance wanted to add shades of gray to the graph screen. In black-and-white photography, the sharpest pictures have many shades of black and gray. Fish in the Lowrance gray line may show as sharply black with a gray center. If the instrument is correctly tuned, their bottom gray line is actually a sandwich—a thin black line, a gray band, and a thin black line. The thickness of the gray band depends on the hardness of the bottom.

Another distortion is illustrated in Figure 14. The transducer gathers all the fish into one line of sight and reports it that way on the receiver screens. Because of this, fish at the same depth may be painted over each other. The three fish at the bottom of the left half of Figure 14 when shifted into straight line-of-transducer sight could have been superimposed upon each other, thus hiding two of them. In this case, each was at a different depth, so all ten fish on the left half of the figure will be painted on the screen in the boat.

Christman, writing in Vexilar's *Seeing Your Underwater World*, summarizes sonar distortion: "The markings of fish on your graph unit are not, necessarily, a completely accurate record of what is actually there in the water, due to the various inaccuracies caused by the way sound behaves in water. (A) There are probably more fish present, separately or in schools, than will be marked at any depth. (B) The fish are probably not bunched together as tightly as they seem to be. (C) The fish you mark are likely to be as much as 5 percent to 10 percent shallower than their markings. (They may be at the exact depth shown by their markings, but they will never be deeper than that, most often shallower.) (D) More times than not, the fish you see will be off to one side or the other from your boat, not directly under it as you might assume them to be. The greater the depth and the wider the cone angle, the greater this difference can be. (E) There are probably more fish in a school than there appears to be. (F) You can't always tell if one fish is bigger than another. (G) Because you may mark a group of fish bunched up and suspended off a breakline or some other structure, but the structure they are relating to doesn't fall within your sound signal cone, you may assume they are just suspended out there in the middle of nowhere in relationship to nothing, obviously an error. (H) You cannot distinguish between different species by the marks they make."

Fishing errors occur because, in our eagerness, we fail to heed Christman's last statement. Thayne Smith laughs about the time he mistook carp recorded on his graph for stripers. While fishing an Oklahoma

How to Use Sonar Graphs and Flashers

impoundment he saw rectangles on his flasher symbolizing large fish. There were stripers in the impoundment, they usually schooled, and he'd never encountered large groups of carp there before. So he fished for stripers, and none of the carp bit. Later, through a friend, he discovered that the bay had been chummed so that carp would gather for an annual Take-a-Boy-Fishing event. In this instance, Smith was using his knowledge of the habitat to interpret the symbols on his flasher. Usually this works. A large fish on the bottom of Lake Huron's Thunder Bay where lake trout and browns have been planted usually is one species or the other, but it could be a Chinook.

There's argument over whether the transducer should be mounted so that the captain can see his own down weight. It's an advantage to see it in comparison with the depth mark and in comparison to fish that are present. The captain can direct the first mate to lower or raise the weight and the trolled lure in accord with his fish sightings on the graph. On the other hand, the long, continuous line the down weight makes can obscure fish and may sometimes be confused with the bottom mark. In my opinion this far outweighs the thrill of seeing fish take the lure or follow. A compromise is to locate the transducer so it paints only one down weight.

Sonars work best when the transducer is correctly mounted. The Lowrance operation manual for the Fish Lo-K-Tor, Model LFG 205, ex-

A bass invades the cockpit to inspect the Lowrance LRG 1510B graph that inspected him. The graph is aimed at the starboard-corner down weight; the graph painted this fish just before it took.

plains how to select the transducer location and gives three methods of mounting. The transducer face (if it's mounted outside the boat hull) or the hull area through which it sends (if it's inside the boat hull) must maintain water contact at all times the unit is in operation. If water contact is broken, the sonar signal will not be sent. If the water that makes contact is full of air bubbles, cavitation noise signals and a reduction in the strength of the signal may result. The transducer should not be located in a place that is out of water when the boat is planing. The transducer cable should not be routed near objects that would damage it or objects laced with other electrical cables.

Through-the-hull sending is not recommended for steel or aluminum boats. It works well in fiberglass hulls, but the point of installation should be inspected for air bubbles that sometimes are trapped in fiberglass material. A test run with the transducer temporarily mounted should remove doubt about the presence of air bubbles. Furthermore, through-the-hull mounting is not recommended for fiberglass hulls having foam, balsa wood, other flotation materials, or a dead-air space between an inner and outer hull.

Transom mount with wedge forward is best for steel, aluminum or wooden hulls or when through-the-hull sending is not practical. Transom mount with point forward is best when the dead rise of the hull exceeds 10 degrees.

Transducers that are mounted outside the hull should be periodically cleaned with soap and water or very fine steel wool to remove the soil and dirt film that may reduce sensitivity or block sending. Remember the flat part is an "eye." Don't scratch it or peel off antifouling coating.

The power your set uses to send can be compared to a radio station's transmitter power. (Remember that for your set the transmitter is right there with you.) Power is the number of watts the station or sonar set is capable of broadcasting. As your car takes the radio farther from the station (similar to the boat taking the sonar over deeper water), you begin to hear a lot of interference and the signal gets weaker. You turn up your radio sensitivity. In the same turn of the dial, you also increase the interference. The noise gets so bad that eventually you switch to a more powerful station. When this happens with a sonar set, you can't switch to a more powerful station because it's your set that is broadcasting! So you may wish that you'd shopped for a set with the power to graph all of your fishing habitats.

Some manufacturers have a knob marked "sensitivity"; others have a knob marked "gain." In sportfishing sonar sets, the two terms are synonymous. In Chapter 2 we discussed sensitivity in VHF-FM radios. In that discussion the term referred to the ability of a set to quiet unwanted interference. In sonar the term refers to amplification, not to quieting. "When I change the gain on a sonar," Ted Hansford, marketing director at Si-Tex, says, "I'm raising and lowering the amplification of the received signal, that is, the echo. Changing the gain does not change the transmitted signal."

In a sonar the inbuilt sensitivity of the crystal in the "eye" of the transducer is more important than raising and lowering amplification. A transducer with a reasonably large crystal coupled with reasonably high power (reasonable in reference to the depth the unit must reach) will obviate sensitivity problems. Increasing and decreasing gain is not a good way to cure economy in transducer selection and power output. Increases in gain leave sets vulnerable to electrical disturbance. Remember that sensitivity or gain is to be low when in shallow water, higher in deeper water.

Suppression devices were first invented to suppress radio interference from spark plugs. There are several electronic devices that can cause interference for sonar sets. Leave the suppression knob turned off until you get unwanted interference. Then turn slowly!

7

The Downrigger— A Trolling Machine

The purpose of a downrigger is to present a lure at a controlled depth to test a captain's ability to locate fish in temperature habitats. If used this way, it's a precision instrument working in harmony with sonar and thermometer. Blind fishing with a downrigger does not ensure presentation to a fish's mouth.

A downrigger is a fishing machine having four major parts—a pulley assembly, a down weight, a release, and a counter. (See Figure 15.) The pulley assembly includes a boom, a cable, two pulleys, a brake, a clutch, and the stand that supports them. Its purpose is to raise and lower the down weight without injury to the operator and, when clutch-equipped, to allow cable to pay out when the down weight becomes snagged on an underwater object. The down weight is a trolling weight to which fishing lines and other devices may be attached. It ensures controlled-depth fishing and thermometer insertion. The release is a device that holds the fishline and lure on the down weight or cable until the force of a fish's strike releases it. Several releases called "stackers" can be mounted one above the other so that one down weight or its cable can troll several lines and lures. The counter reads out the number of feet the down weight is hanging below the arm. Thus lure, sonar, and temperature depths can be coordinated.

Downriggers were created by Great Lakes inventors because salmonids imported from the Pacific and Atlantic Oceans suspended in mid-

The Downrigger—
a Trolling Machine

dle water where they could not be taken with long, weighted lines. A weighted line is reasonably efficient in upper waters to 20 feet. It's also reasonably efficient when bumping bottom in lower waters. It's horribly inefficient, because of line bellying and the effect of water pressures and currents, at middle depths. It was generally recognized that more precise trolling presentation to fish's mouths was needed at all water depths. The downrigger satisfies this need.

Why are long, weighted, trolling lines inefficient? First, because line weight and trolling speed can only be adjusted to achieve a guesstimated depth. The weight the line contributes varies by length and diameter. The size of the lure complicates the equation. Second, the equation requires long line that tangles at turns when more than one rod is set. Third, long lines do not synch with sonar depths. You can't put a depth counter on a long line. A down weight on a cable that does very little bellying eliminates all these variables by firmly escorting the line and lure to a counted depth. Of course, if the line from down weight to lure is long, the lure may plane up or down from the down-weight depth. But that's variance within the striking range of fish sighted on sonar graphs.

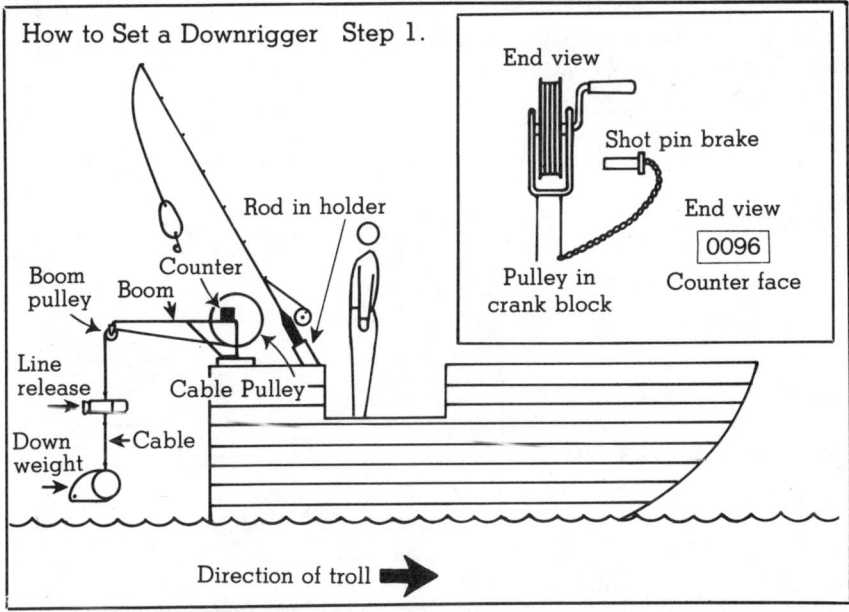

Figure 15. *Step one: The downrigger and rod are set up on the transom gunwale ready to be joined in underwater trolling. The boat is running at trolling speed. How does the captain put the fishing line on a release that's several feet to stern and below the gunwale? How does he avoid falling into the water beneath the running boat? These questions are asked by a captain standing on the deck of a fairly large boat. If he were seated in a 12-foot boat, all he'd have to do is lean over the transom.*

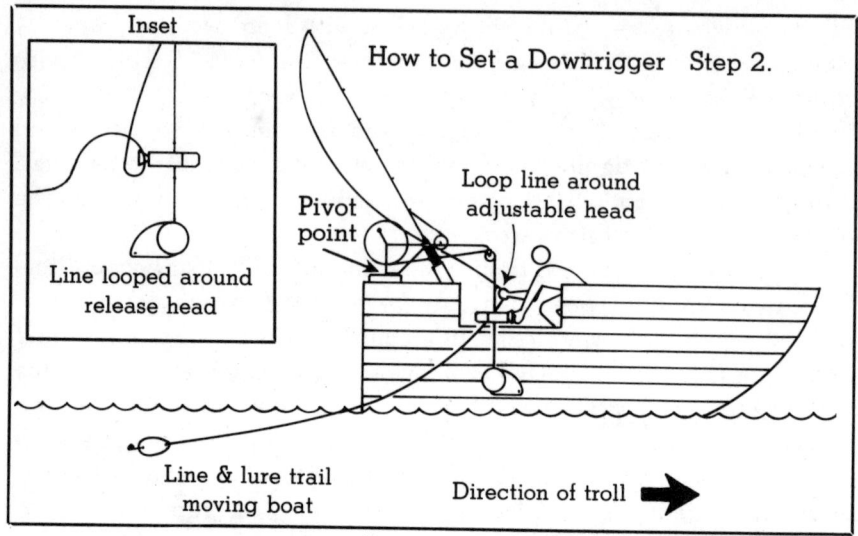

Figure 16. *Step two:* The downrigger boom is pivoted so the down weight and release are either entirely in the boat or dangle near the gunwale. The line is fed off the fishing reel into the water for the estimated distance the lure is to run behind the down weight. The lure will ride near the surface at this time. Its action should be checked. If the captain is using a button-type release, it will be on the line and he'll be holding it while paying line out. In this case, the captain loops the line around the adjustable head. Next he pivots the boom to point sternward over the water.

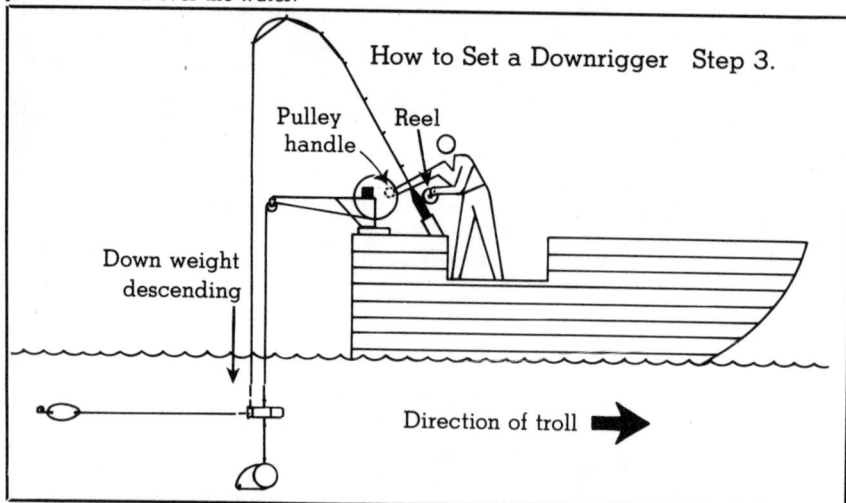

Figure 17. *Step three:* The captain is letting the down weight crank into the water while maintaining tension on the reel so it won't backlash. He's watching the counter for depth. Fishing line is paying off the reel from the pull of the descending down weight. The rod tip will bounce in response to uneven tensions from this pull. A trolling reel can be put into free-spool. If so, finger tension must be maintained on the spool. Another way of letting line pay off the reel is to loosen the drag. If it's not too loose, finger tension need not be maintained.

The Downrigger—
a Trolling Machine

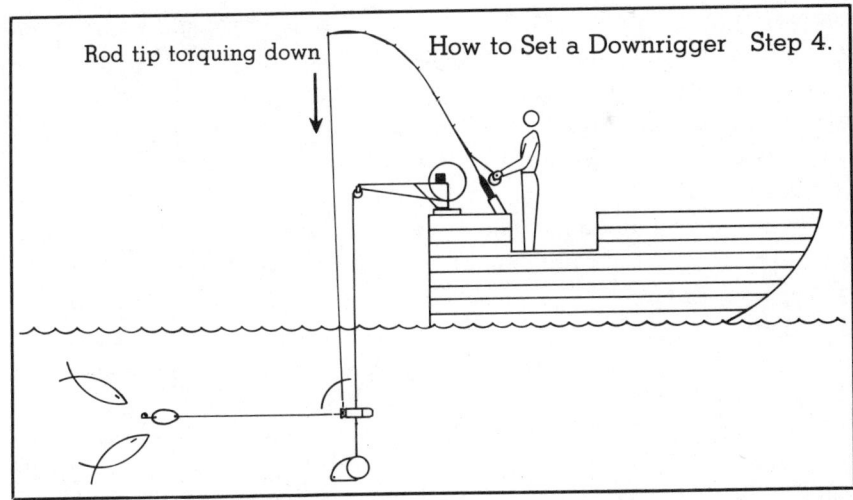

Figure 18. *Step four: The captain is torquing the rod tip down to maintain tension against the release. Remember that the fish may produce slack at point A. Slack lines allow fish to get off, so there should be no slack between the rod tip and release. While torquing, the captain will get the feel of the trolling line and lure. He's now watching the rod tip, ready to cry, "Fish on!" Beneath the water two fish are watching. Will one of them cause the captain more work by tripping the line from the release?*

When coho and Chinook came to Michigan waters, many fishermen began to experiment with rigging down to weights. It was a group challenge. Some of these people were aware of lake trout trolling with weights and metal lines. They know that a lake trout encumbered with a window sash makes a poor antagonist. They went out on Lakes Michigan and Huron with all kinds of devices designed to hold a line where scuba divers and biologists said the fish were swimming. They put their fishing machines together in home workshops. Everyone learned that weights are difficult to raise and lower with hand lines. Pulleys were needed. (See Figure 3.) In San Francisco Bay and in Puget Sound, fishermen also needed pulleys. They had a somewhat different problem. They used a sinker and a sinker release. When the force of a fish's strike opened the release, the sinker dropped to the bottom, and the fish could be fought with only the encumbrance of the release device. But as lead became more expensive (the sinkers ranged from ¼ ounce to 10 pounds), fishermen attached a line to the sinker and pulled it up after fighting the fish. They also needed pulleys to raise heavy weights from deep depths. In the Great Lakes, pulleys from old washing machines and boat winches appeared on the back ends of boats, pieces of railroad iron and lead ingots dangled from them, and arms designed to keep the pulleys from scarring and marring the boat transoms were also jury-rigged out of wood, metal tubing, and whatever. Michigan's scrap piles became waterborne. Alligator clips, shirt buttons, West Coast–style sinker releases, and rubber bands were the first releases. Fishermen carried wrenches, hacksaws, and sewing materials in their tackle boxes. It was all quite creative, but a lot of fouled gear and foul-mouthed remarks became commonplace above the swimming salmon.

Discipline was brought to the armada of gadgeteers by a surgical-instrument manufacturer and inventor of fishing lures, Jim Walker (he was later joined by Mike Lummis); a scuba diver, Jon Emery, Jr., teamed with a mechanical engineer, his father, Jon Emery, Sr.; a custom coating construction manager, Richard McEwen; and a tool and die maker, Jim Rieth. These four pioneers brought the early Michigan downriggers from experimental state to factory production. Jack King, a design engineer for Shaw Walker in Muskegon, Michigan, designed a downrigger that Luhr Jensen, a West Coast tackle manufacturer, produces. Jerry Harsch, a South Haven, Michigan, boat outfitter, designed a downrigger that the Plath Company, another West Coast company, now produces. So six of the companies now producing downriggers were guided by the creativity of Michigan inventors. Mike Lummis was active in a group that bought out Jim Walker and operates Pacific Atlantic Products, which produces Walker downriggers. In Kalamazoo, Michigan, Jim Rieth is president of the Riviera Marine and Tackle Company, Grand Rapids, Michigan, which produces Riviera downriggers. Jon Emory, Jr., is president of Big Jon, Traverse City, Michigan. Richard McEwen is president of Mac-Jac, Muskegon, Michigan. All of these men were active fishermen who caught coho fever and set to sea with pulleys, weights, and lures. They also spent considerable time at their drawing boards, in lending institutions, in patent attorneys' offices, and in their factories.

There were many others, among them two men from Racine, Wisconsin, who produced the Indian City downrigger, and a man from Portage, Michigan, who produced a downrigger made mostly of wood. Today, several other firms manufacture downriggers, including K-Line Industries, Holland, Michigan/producing Jim Kammeraad's Bonny-Invader/and Proos in Grand Rapids, Michigan. We cannot describe them all, so we'll mostly present the works and thoughts of the Michigan pioneers and their West Coast affiliates—Luhr Jensen, Hood River, Oregon, and Plath, Portland, Oregon.

It's logical to assume that there was West Coast influence in the invention of downriggers. Salmon imported from the Pacific Ocean catalyzed their creation, and West Coast commercial fishermen developed a way of raising and lowering weights for fishing with long lines called Gurdies.

The Downrigger— a Trolling Machine

(Gurdies do not have releases.) But most of the pioneering Michigan manufacturers say they were not influenced by West Coast ideas. Mac-Jac, Riviera, Walker, and Big Jon all report that they were not influenced by knowledge of Gurdies. Jerry Harsch, from whom Plath bought rights, does say that he was aware of commercial Gurdies, and had them in mind while he was creating his prototype. Harsch lived on the West Coast from 1959 to 1965.

Of course this idea of rigging down was possibly invented and reinvented in many places, but credit for the flowering of downriggers into a sportfishing device can be given to a group of Michigan fishermen who started tinkering in their home workshops. Some of them went on to manufacture a four-part machine. Bruce L. Wing, an oceanography investigator for the NOA Auke Bay, Alaska, Fisheries Laboratory, says that when he was a boy, Puget Sound hand trollers "used a rope, window sash weight, and clothespin catch." Probably other examples can be cited. But the fruition of tinkering into a four-part manufactured machine occurred in Michigan because of the interest in controlled depth and temperature fishing created by the importation of salmon. No attempt is being made to figure out who was the first among this group of home workshop creators. At about the same period, several brought their work to factory production.

Big Jon Emory, a scuba diver, aided by his father's mechanical engineering know-how and backed by businessmen including Dr. John Spencer, has become a leader among Traverse City fishermen. When the salmon came to Michigan, he owned a dive shop, taught scuba diving courses, and searched for wrecked ships with a Lowrance sonar. He saw that salmon suspended at various depths and, from diving, realized they were at various temperature levels. He found an old V-belt pulley, fitted it to a stand, and mounted it on the transom of his boat for lowering and raising down weights. "But this was not our major breakthrough," he says. "Down weights have been around a long time. Dad and I struggled to develop a release that would work along with the down weight." (See Figure 4.) "We conceived the first release mechanism that used a clip," he explained. Meanwhile, Jim Walker invented a release that didn't require a clip. The Big Jon Company has recently brought out another release that doesn't require a clip, the Free'N easy.

Jim Rieth made his living from the Riviera Die & Tool business; fishing was his hobby. He also realized that the salmon were "stratified," so he began tinkering in his factory. "I saw a collage of junk mounted on boats," he says. "Bicycle wheels and pie pans." He remembers that in November 1968 he and Big Jon displayed downriggers in adjoining booths in a tackle show in Grand Rapids, Michigan. "This was the first time downriggers were displayed for commercial sale," he said.

Richard McEwen was the manager of Custom Coating Company, which formed a division to produce the Mac-Jac, which he brought out. He was influenced in his early thinking by the knowledge that the Indians hand-lined for fish on the Great Lakes. His prototype was made of pipe fittings and washing-machine pulleys. He says that his first releases were made of alligator clips and shirt buttons.

Jim Walker, surgical-instrument producer, says he started with a window sash and a boat winch. He designed the Walker release now sold with Walker downriggers of aluminum and stainless steel. He's the inventor of the Little Abalure, which takes its name from abalone shell. Walker was joined by Mike Lummis in 1971. They worked together to design their first electric unit, and in 1974 the Lummis group bought Walker out. In 1976 Lummis redesigned their unit, and in 1980 brought out a new clutch that lowers the down weight, obviating down cranking on the manual models.

Phil Jensen, president of Luhr Jensen, realized there was a market for downriggers because sales of lead weights from his company skyrocketed as coho fishing increased in Michigan. He also heard the complaints of San Francisco Bay fishermen who needed pulleys to get their down weights back. "We decided there was a market in the Great Lakes, the Sound, and the Bay," he says. For a year they sold Indian City downriggers, but after deciding that these well-bult units were too costly to produce because they required heavy aluminum castings, Jensen found out about Jack King. King had developed new lightweight structures through his work designing chairs for Shaw Walker. Luhr Jensen bought rights to produce his downrigger design. Jensen himself worked on the design for a pear-shaped down weight.

You may ask, "Why all the expense of the machinery—pulleys, cables, arms, and so on? Why not attach a release to a down weight and raise and lower the weight with a rope tied to the boat transom?"

Hang out your third-story window and raise and lower an 8-pound weight with 20 feet of rope a few times. Then go to an office building and raise and lower the weight with 100 feet of rope. Get rope burn? Bang the weight on the side of the building? Lose control and drop the thing on somebody's head? These problems become a little more complicated when raising and lowering in water. "So we need a pulley," you concede. "We'll rig one on the transom." But pulleys follow their own laws, you'll discover. Eight pounds on 20 feet of rope will run wild, causing the pulley (actually a winch) crank to rotate dangerously. And the rope gets wet;

The Downrigger— a Trolling Machine 67

the down weight catches on the transom and the engine. You need a cable instead of a rope, a boom with a pulley at its end, and a brake on the winch-pulley to stop it when the proper depth is reached. Next the down weight catches on a bottom rock, you aren't fast enough with the throttle, and the boat momentum stretches the cable to the breaking point. You have just lost one down weight. You'll lose others, but not so many after a clutch that allows the cable to slip is installed. The downriggers in the sporting-goods shops are worth their money!

Anything that stops a winch-pulley from turning is a brake. Shot pins are inserted through a hole in the frame and a corresponding hole in the winch-pulley rim. Luhr Jensen uses a hinged tongue. The tip of the tongue can be raised to stick into the winch rim. Cam gear teeth fitting into corresponding gear teeth in the winch rim are used by Bonny-Invader. These are all manual devices requiring hand setting. Electric models have an interior "park" gear.

Clutches operate somewhat like the drag on a free-spooling fly reel. If a down weight catches on an underwater object, the winch will turn and the cable will pay out. Some clutches (Walker's is an example) can be tightened like the star drag on a reel to a tension point that will hold a down weight at any stopping point. When untorqued (Walker ads say "unreeled"), the winch will unreel or allow cable to pay off as the down weight lowers. When you're working a boat and tending four downriggers, a clutch creates much happiness.

Electric models will shut themselves off when they're raised. An electric heat-sensing device "notices" that the motor is still working and does the job. This means that if you're playing a fish, all you need do to get the downrigger cable and weight out of tangling way is to touch the up switch with one finger. This creates still more happiness.

Clutches and electric motors stop frantic fishing frenzies. Imagine yourself and a captain working a boat with no other help. You do not have an autopilot and there's wind and a slight chop. The boat wants to yaw around a bit. It's legal for you to have two rods apiece set, so four hand-crank downriggers' cables are singing in the water. You've just joined three other boats who are figure-eighting over a school of coho. Two of your rods pop, so you have two fish to play and two down weights to hand-crank to surface. OK. One of you handles two rods, keeping proper tension on the fish, while the other cranks up one down weight, races to the wheel, then races back to get the other down weight up. It's half up and rod number three pops up. Your companion sets that hook, starts fighting that fish, backs to the wheel rod in hand, and avoids collision with another boat that's having the same kind of action. There's no hope of getting the remaining down weights up, and who's going to net the fish? Bingo—rod four pops, and you can't do anything about it. The fish gets off. You lose one of the three fish you've been playing, net two, stay on course, and start resetting your hand cranks. You did well. But if you'd had electrics you might have bagged all four fish.

Imagine now that you had no counters on the hand cranks in this situation. Would you have remembered to count the number of upward turns? Would you have remembered what you counted? There's not much we can say about the counters themselves. Most of them work fairly well; all they have to do is rotate printed numbers. They help in two other ways. (1) They tell the depth of your downrigged thermometer, so you know how deep to troll when you find the desired temperature habitat.(2) They synch well with the depth scale on the sonar. If you see a fish opposite the 20-foot mark on your graph, all you need do is turn the downrigger crank until its counter nears 20. You don't have to think about it, and you may be thinking about making a turn, avoiding a boat, or taking a bearing on the Jonestown water tower.

The rod tip in Figure 18 is being bent toward the underwater down weight because the reel will torque or turn until the line tension is near the pop-up point of the release. When a fish strikes a rod that isn't downrigged (a flat line), it pulls the rod tip downward. But when a fish strikes against a release, the torqued rod tip pops upward because it has also been released. Not all pop-ups are caused by fish. When taking up lines or changing lures the fisherman pops the line loose before raising the down weight. This avoids line and line-cable tangles. So releases must release from many angles—both from the place the fish swims and from the place the fisherman stands. Jim Kammeraad, creator of the Bonny-Invader, says in an unpublished manuscript entitled "Downrigger Trolling" that it's possible to invent releases that the fish can easily pop underwater, but the fisherman cannot pop from the deck.

Releases do many other jobs. They must be gentle to fishing lines. They should have a tension device that allows them to be set for the strike of both light and heavy fish. And the device should take a large range of line sizes. Releases should be created with species behavior in mind. Lake trout, for example, may be followers that bite the hook and swim along instead of popping the line loose from the release. Salmon on their spawning migration develop hard mouths and may pop the line loose without setting the hook. Muskie always have hard jaws and often clamp down on a hook hard enough to prevent it from moving into a set. The line will pop out of the release, the fisherman will seize the rod in the proper upsweeping motion, and the muskie will open his mouth, releasing a hook

The Downrigger—
a Trolling Machine

that isn't hooked. Releases must be versatile.

A release that will not release from the fisherman's end and often fails to release at the fish's end is the sinker release/down weight combination. A wire with a ring on the trailing end is fastened to a down weight; the sinker release clamps into the ring just as it would on a sinker. Unfortunately the fish often cannot release the mechanism because the angle of force is not correct, and the down weight, which is not a sinker, does not help by giving gravitational pull. Because a sinker release opens from only one end the fisherman can't pop it. The down weight with line, lure, and release attached must be raised to separate them. This creates tangles and bad tempers.

Another ancient release that seems too simple to be true really does

A pair of lake trout taken out of South Haven with rubber-band releases.

work—the rubber band! Lay the fishing line down on the rubber band and at right angles to it. You now have two loops—one on either side of the line. Pull one through the other. You now have one loop. Put it over any hook that won't foul. A short wire leader with a swivel and snap at both ends can be attached to the down weight. A notch cut with a coping-saw blade in an "Auto Track" rudder will retain the rubber-band loop. A duo-lock snap that fits the retaining hole on the rudder of many down weights combined with a pull test snap for the rubber-band loop will work for many situations. Remember to change the rubber-band size to suit the size of the fish. Charter Captain Torba uses size 16 when fishing for salmon and trout out of New Buffalo, Michigan. Rubber bands rig easily and pop cleanly. There's no fumbling with a widget! Charter Captain Joe Kimmerly says that nearly all boats running out of St. Joseph use them. Rubber bands can be stacked. Caution: If a rubber band is too heavy it will stretch instead of breaking. In such cases the fish may fight the rubber band, causing odd rod-tip telegraphing. The captain seeing this may say, "Another damned rubber-band fight!" It's like using a Pacific Ocean commercial fisherman's rubber snubber. The reason the captain swears is that the fish and its stretched rubber band have to be raised simultaneously with the down weight, and some horrendous tangles often ensue. So use light rubber bands. Even if you decide against rubber-band releases, a few light ones in the tackle box are good insurance against losing or breaking releases.

The alligator clip is another ancient release that hangs on. Alligator clips are used to clamp wire onto electrical terminals and leads. Twenty-amp clips are equipped with rubber pads, a short length of cable, and a swivel snap. Fabricated in many home workshops and sold by Ricker's Tackle Manufacturing Company in Sebewaing, Michigan, they make good releases. Bruce DeShano says they telegraph lure action to the rod tip more directly than other releases. Figure 19 shows how alligator releases cause the rod tip to travel when a fish is in the act of popping the line out of the release or when a fish hitchhikes. (A hitchhiker is a fish that takes the lure and swims along at trolling speed without releasing the line. Small fish may do this.) "If you're dragging a hitchhiker," DeShano says, "you probably won't take more fish because he's sending panic signals through his lateral lines."

The button release has many brand names. A doughnut-shaped piece of plastic with a female outer rim that will press into retaining notches or clips is the major part in these releases. The doughnut, which succeeded the shirt buttons originally used in the Traverse City area, slips up and down the line and is placed above and before the lure. On Bonny-Invader

The Downrigger—
a Trolling Machine

releases, it slips into a clip that is the trailing end of a clip/duo-lock snap assembly. The snap is attached to the Bonny-Invader down-weight rudder. On Mac-Jac the same rig is used with a slightly different snap, and efficient stacking is obtained by using a cable snap. Mac-Jac calls these Cable Release 455. They pop out at 6 pounds pull and can be adjusted to 4 pounds or less.

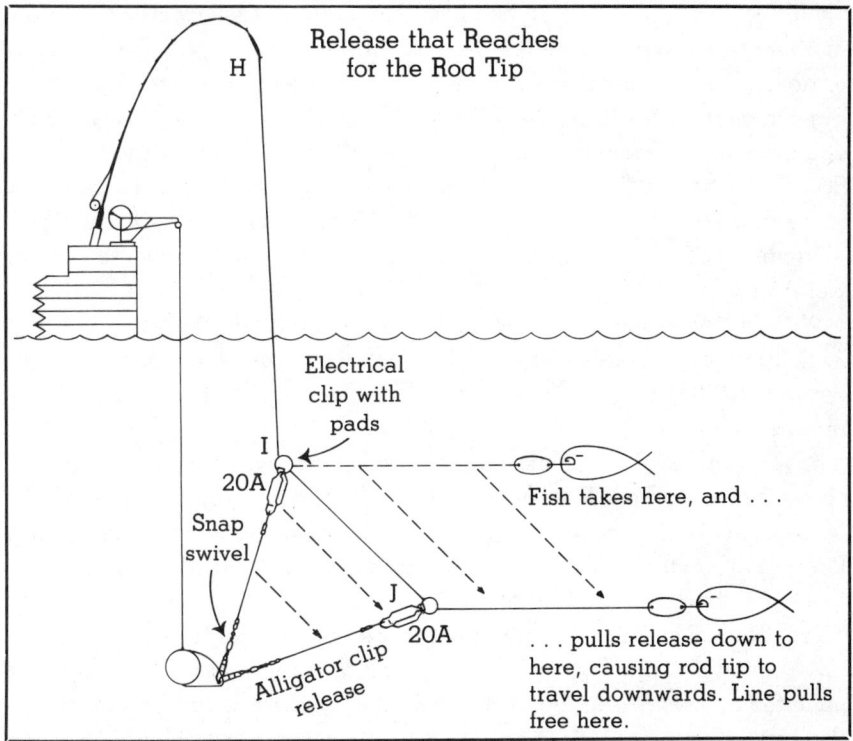

Figure 19. *The alligator-clip release can be purchased at a tackle store or assembled in the home workshop from an electrical clip, a snap swivel, and a length of leader cable. Unless the rod to which the release is torqued is very stiff, it will help the fisherman read the rod tip for strikes and hitchhiking fish. When the rod is torqued, the release cable will extend upward as in position I. After a fish takes, the release will pull to a position near J, causing the rod tip H to dip downward, signaling to the fisherman tending rods.*

The Luhr Jensen "Auto Track" release is a rudder with snap-in notches for releasing buttons at 2, 4, 6, and 8 pounds pull. The rudder tracks the lure and accurately points the button at the striking fish's line of force, so the system works smoothly. The tracking rudder is a help in heavy seas, big swells, and currents.

All of the buttons are pressed into place after giving the line a few twists. They are reliable and foulproof. Their disadvantage is that they are always getting lost. Both my dog and my grandchild have swallowed them. They disappear into crevices, and passengers take them home.

At Big Jon the barrel-and-clip release succeeded the button-and-clip device during the evolution of their prototype. The clip has a ring, which looks like a button, in one end for the line. It isn't. It's a ring. The *clip* presses into a notch on a dumbbell-shaped milled barrel. The barrel has a choice of three notches that, because they're progressively slightly larger in diameter, provide a different release pull. Use two clips on two notches to get higher-poundage pull. Mate the two clips with a large split ring. Big Jon barrel-clip releases are made for stacking on the down-weight cable and for attachment at the cable end above the down weight. LR 800 P.L.—it doesn't have any other name—is for the end of the cable. It has a ring in each end of the barrel. The Freeloader release has a right-angle bracket at each end of the barrel for sliding up and down the down-weight cable.

With button releases the button slides up and down the line. With Big Jon clip-and-barrel releases, the clip ring slides up and down the line. In both, twist the line a few times before popping it into place on the retainer.

Several releases on the market have a tension-setting device. These include Big Jon's Free'N easy, the Walker adjustable line release, Luhr Jensen's magnetic release, Riviera's adjustable tension release, and Penn's Fathomtrol release. Both the Riviera and Penn releases have the tension setting mounted on the down weight.

Free'N easy has a flip-up pin that can be adjusted for tension. Wrap the line around the pin and flip down to lock in trolling position. The pin is mounted diagonally on the hypotenuse of a right-angle rudder that tracks the lure. It is mounted at cable end above the down weight. On the Walker release, the line wraps around a plunger that can be adjusted for tension. Walker releases can be mounted at cable end or they'll slide up and down the down-weight cable for easy stacking. Neither Free'N easy nor the Walker release require a doughnut or tab on the line. No doughnut hunts!

On Luhr Jensen's magnetic release, the button is one pole of the magnetic field. When running, stick extra buttons on a piece of metal fixed to the transom. When not running, keep them in a cloth bag. These are not soft chewables like the plastic ones enjoyed by my dog and grandchild!

Riviera and Penn releases have the tension side-mounted on the down weight. These well-scaled units provide good tracking and good tension setting. Of course, if you lose or misplace your down weight you've lost the tension-setting half of your release. Neither your dog nor your grandchildren will swallow this side, but sharks do eat down weights, so there's another hang-up!

Down weights must annoy fish. They reflect light, make shadows, create a wake, and raise sonic sound from their bulk and from the vibrating downrigger cables. They're being hauled through the fish's line of sight and "radar." Although they don't spook the fish we catch, they probably spook fish we don't catch. Generations of fish may grow up to be down-weight shy. We can't avoid much of this, but we can camouflage the weights in the same deep-sea colors God provides for the fish—a green back and a silver body. Viewed from above, a fish's green back blends in with the green waters and bottom below. Viewed from below, a fish's silver belly blends with the lighted sky. Some captains move in the opposite direction by painting their weights in bright colors, hoping to attract fish to the trailing lures.

Down weights do "lead-pencil" boat transoms and decks. Covering weights with vinyl stops this, but the vinyl sheds camouflage paint.

Shape affects the way down weights perform in the water. There are three general designs—round or cannonball-shaped, streamlined or fish-shaped, and pear-shaped. All three have fins or rudders. Round weights follow the boat well and stop and turn with it. They crank up easily. Streamlined weights offer less water resistance and probably follow the boat better. But they don't stop and turn well. Instead, they continue of their own momentum on the pulled line of force and create tangles.

A rudder attached to the cannonball shape is the solution to down-weight hydrodynamics offered by Big Jon and Mac-Jac. Flattening the round ball's sides and adding a rudder is the solution offered by Bonny-Invader in the K-Line factory. Riviera uses a torpedo shape with an arch-shaped rudder. Theirs is a hollow shell that may be filled with varying weights determined by the size of lead balls. Proos has a solid torpedo-shaped weight. Phil Jensen felt that he'd sell his weights in the coastal part of Luhr Jensen's distribution area. "Lead is expensive to ship," he explains. So he designed for ocean usage. "We troll faster on the coast and in more currents," he says. His is pear-shaped with a down-sweeping fin at the rear. "It tracks well without fouling and provides proper streamlining," Jensen says.

Richard McEwen at Mac-Jac cautions captains to troll weights of the same design. "Different designs track differently, and a mixture of tracking planes will create tangles at turns," he says.

Most captains carry two weight ranges with them. They may use 4- and

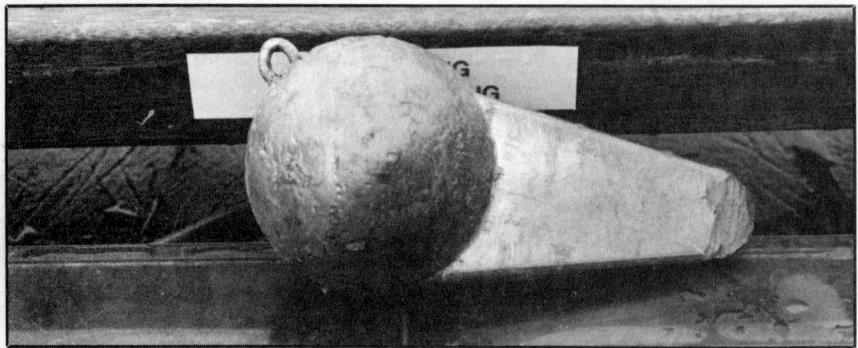

A rock-scarred homemade down weight made from salvaged lead. The ball-with-fin shape is popular with home weight casters. Note that the wire-reinforced eye is at 45-degree angle to plumb of ball.

5-pound weights when fishing shallow and 7-, 10-, and 12-pound when fishing deep. However, fishing for smaller species of fish doesn't necessarily mean using mini-weights. Joe Hughes, Rebel professional fisherman, likes plenty of weight even for shallow water. He uses Riviera shells filled with smaller lead balls for stripers in deep water and for bass in shallow water. He finds that the Riviera release on the shell works well for both heavy and light fish.

Some down weights have planes on the side that aid tracking. But the planes create resistance to upward pull, so hand-cranking them from 100 feet can be a chore! Walker's weight with side planes is cast in the shape of a fish and nicknamed Herbie.

Because lead is expensive, you may want to salvage your own lead and cast your own weights. Lead is where you find it. Two sources are wheel weights and discarded wet-cell batteries. Be cautious about the acid and noxious fumes in batteries. Break the battery up and let the acid drain off. Neutralize. When melting the remainder, various noxious gases may be driven off. Melt under a hood or in the open air. You'll need plumber's pot for melting and a ladle for pouring. Wear gloves.

What molds should we pour into? Mechanics have all kinds of ways of making molds, but down-weight molds can be bought. One place is R-L-M Sales Company in Tualatin, Oregon.

When fishing, a downrigger is married to a rod and reel. As in all marriages, annoying tangles threaten the ecstasy of perfect union. Obviously the down weight dangling over the transom is supposed to sink the lure. Obviously the line must be put into the release. But how do we get the dangling down weight and the release into the boat? Figures 15 through 18 show how to set a line with a downrigger. In Figure 15 all is made ready. This setup shows a hand-crank downrigger equipped with a counter and a rod with a trolling reel. Electric downriggers are easier to set. Spinning reels provide slightly different setting problems. The easiest way for the captain to attach the line to the release is to jump out and run around behind the boat. Unfortunately that won't work, so the downrigger, unless it has a very short arm, is equipped with a pivot to turn release, down weight, and cable inside the boat. (See Figure 16.) After the line is attached to the release, the boom is swung back over the water. All during setting the boat is running, and at this point, the line and lure are in the water following the boat. The captain must be certain the line doesn't tangle as the boom is pivoted. He'll be checking to see whether he's attached the line firmly enough to prevent water drag from popping it loose from the release. He'll be watching the lure to be certain it hasn't fouled. Now he's ready to take step 3, illustrated in Figure 17. If the captain were operating an electric downrigger, he'd be pushing a button with his left hand instead of minding a crank turning at the pull of a down weight. In this case, he's helped by a counter. If there were no counter he'd count the number of crank turns to estimate depth of down weight. If the captain were operating a spinning reel, he'd have the bail open (unless working against the drag) and his fingers would mind the line as it payed off the reel flange. In some instances, lowering against the drag on a spinning reel will cause monofilament to stretch and later tangle. It depends somewhat on the quality of the line and the nature of the reel.

Lowering requires two hands. The captain begins lowering after he's determined that the down weight, cable, and line will not foul as they enter the water. As he starts lowering, his eye goes to the tip of the rod to be certain the fish line hasn't wrapped itself around the rod. Then he notices whether the line is paying out of all the guides. If it isn't, it may have fouled on the reel. While his eye is working and his left hand is playing the cable crank, his right hand is playing the reel. He's concerned about backlash. He watches the counter to obtain correct depth. No wonder the captain looks as if he's playing a harp while lowering. It's not an easy task.

At step 4 the captain's mood shifts. There may be a fish on at any moment. No one yells "Fish on!" more loudly than the man who has the rod pop up as he's torquing down. This frequently happens when we're lowering into a school of fish sighted on sonar. After torquing, the captain will check the drag setting and make certain that all gear is clear of the downrigger and rod and reel. He looks at the rod tip to see whether its vibrations indicate any fouling of lure action. He looks closely at the

Boom clearance for this Big Jon side rigger was obtained by mounting bracket at a 45-degree angle. Down cable passes behind lake trout to weight storage port. Fish taken in midwinter on Lake Tahoe at 100 feet in 37-degree water. Note Fenwick IGFA rod and Penn 349 reel set with dodger and fly. (Courtesy Skeeter Rubins.)

The Downrigger—
a Trolling Machine

A method of mounting downriggers on a low transom. These manual Rivieras are mounted on a plank installed above the standard fittings on the boat.

downrigger to be certain it's not sneaking more cable into the water. Is the downrigger brake correctly set? Did the free-spool mechanism click into place?

When the rod pops up, the hook has to be set, the rod handed to someone, the down weight cranked back up, and the fish fought and netted. Then it all has to be done over again.

In the line drawings we've shown representatives of the two major kinds of releases—doughnut or button and adjustable. At step 2 the captain is putting line into a Walker release. Figure 4 shows a Big Jon doughnut (this one's actually shaped like a bead) release. Twist the line a few turns before inserting a doughnut into the clip. The same instructions apply for the Mac-Jac button and the Luhr Jensen rudder releases. When using a Riviera release, put a loop into the release—do not wrap the line around the release. When using the Big Jon Free'N easy, wrap the line around the snap-out pin, and snap down.

Mounting the downriggers requires planning. Many boats carry four of them. You'll make quicker turns and have fewer tangles if all four are mounted in line on the gunwale over the transom from port to starboard corners. Another mounting pattern is two short-arm riggers on the stern and two long-arm riggers on starboard and port gunwales. The long arms should be mounted as far to the stern as possible. (They should be farther back than broad on the quarter, and therefore they're not quarter rods. They're usually called "side riggers.") The reason for this is that a turning boat rotates on its centerpoint. Downriggers placed toward that centerpoint, abeam, will drag their cables across the path of cables at stern. If you've already mounted your downriggers and the side riggers are fouling on turns or strikes, one of the three following suggestions made by Jeff Heintz, captain of the *Linda Sue*, in a feature in the June 1979 issue of *Great Lakes Steelheader* may work for you: "Move your side riggers rearward next to the rear downriggers, extend the booms outward on the side downriggers, or use weights that can be made to track right or left by bending the tail fin." Downriggers mounted at the side should be set deeper than those on the stern. If your boat has swim ladders, engines, and other equipment taking up stern space, you may want to choose from a variety of arm lengths offered by manufacturers. It's best to plan for working space at the deck before the transom. Can the downriggers be rotated and cranked without banging into other gear or the boat? Is there room enough to let several operators work at once? Do you need arms that tilt when you dock? These are the questions; you and your boat style provide the answers.

8
The Trolling Trinity

"Graph, thermometer, downriggers," Stan Lievense muttered. He was adjusting tiedown straps on the Starcraft, kicking trailer tires, and hollering at his wife for a thermos bottle. He counted off on his fingers: "Downrigger, thermometer, graph!"

"The trolling trinity," I said.

"You and your theology," Lievense said. He got under the wheel of the state van and cranked the engine.

"Peter was a theologian, and he caught a lot of fish," I said. Lievense couldn't reply because Mary, his wife, came across the lawn with a picnic basket and the thermos bottle. We were heading for Hammond Bay on the northern Michigan shore of Lake Huron to take in-migrating Chinook lying in the Ocqueoc River current. We'd heard they were assembled near the river mouth waiting to run to upstream spawning gravel.

As we rolled along Highway M23, Lievense agreed with my term. "You know, they are interrelated—a trinity," he said. I was drowsing in the mid-September sunshine and didn't answer. The same sun that put me to sleep warmed Hammond Bay during the four hours it took us to make the run to the ramp near the U.S. Fish and Wildlife Research Station on Hammond Bay. After we got the boat into the water, Lievense took the surface temperature with his Thermo-spotter: 63 degrees at shore. "Damned hot!" he said. It was 58 degrees over 50-foot depth.

With engines roaring we ran to the Ocqueoc current influence, where

A grand slam—steelhead, brown, lake trout, coho, Chinook. (Courtesy Michigan Travel Commission.)

An 18-pound Chinook being netted in Hammond Bay, Lake Huron. (Courtesy Michigan Travel Commission.)

Lievense switched the graph on. The depths ran 15 feet, 18 feet, 22 feet, 18 feet; then 30 feet. Lievense threw the engine into neutral and dropped the weighted thermometer sensor into the lake. "Temperature's good here," he said. It was 56 degrees. I was watching the graph. "No fish," I said. Lievense swung the boat to graph the habitat north of the river influence, then zigged to graph south of the current. We sat there letting the transducer be an underwater eye. We got a good view of a boring, smooth bottom and located several submerged objects. To me they looked like long, fuzzy blurs. "Kinda cylindrical," Lievense said. On the graph they were square—probably sunken logs. Further zigzagging got us into 50-foot depth, where we saw no fish but found the water to be a degree colder. "Odd!" Lievense said. We set the down weights at 40 feet and swung the boat to zigzag toward the river mouth. We knew that there probably would be Chinook waiting to run upriver to spawn somewhere in the current influence. The beach, sand dunes, and trees reflected clearly in the full, midday sunlight. I took off my shirt. The water temperature got successively warmer as we neared shore. I stood by the downrigger cranks to raise the down weights as Lievense called the depths. At 30 feet he forgot, but, seeing the rod tips telegraphing the hop, hop, hop of the down weights on bottom sand, I gave the pulleys a few cranks, and retorqued the rod tips. For every "upward" turn of the downrigger pulleys, there must be an equal "downward" turn of the reel handles. At 16-foot depth the graph painted several fish shapes, and they spooked from the boat. The water temperature was 60 degrees. "We won't catch any of them," Lievense said.

We rigged Sea Skees on rods set to point abeam—both starboard and port. These were to reach out to take fish the boat didn't spook. (We didn't have outriggers.) We continued to graph a few fish but got no takes. Various trolling patterns spooked more fish. We put Dardevle flutter spoons on the starboard downriggers and Luhr Jensen J-Plugs on the port downriggers. We managed 12-foot depth all right without dragging anything or tangling. Lievense, turning to run along shore, held the keel over 18-foot depth, which put the starboard Skee over about 12-foot depth. After running about a quarter of a mile, he swung out into the lake, and I began lowering down weights and lures. While we were figure-eighting back and at right angles to the river current at 18-foot depth, the starboard Dardevle took a fish. I grabbed the rod as Lievense shouted, "Fish on!" The fish, heading toward the river mouth, peeled off line in a magnificent run that ended in a high leap. "Chinook!" Lievense yelled. It was a fairly dark fish and came readily to the net. I had to work the rod against the fish's weight, but the warm temperature gave us a sluggish fish.

"Time for a change of habitat," Lievense said. He studied NOA nautical chart 14886 while I untangled the fish and the net and got the dangling down weights out of the water.

"There's a deep pothole near river influence northeast of the old light house," Lievense said, "but I can't find it on the chart." We powered over there, found the pothole with the graph (70-foot depth), noted that there were no fish, and stopped to put the thermometer down. "Great temperature," Lievense said. Pressing the red Thermospotter button with his thumb, he held the dial toward me—55 degrees. We graphed around in a figure-eight with the down weights set maximum, 65 feet, raising to 40 feet and lowering as we came back over the pothole. Nothing.

"The chart shows a drop-off about a mile north of Hammond Village," Lievense said. "It's about 3 miles northeast of the Ocqueoc and out of the river-current influence, but maybe the Chinook have parked there."

On arrival at the spot, the graphs showed 30 feet, 40 feet, then 91 feet, followed by readings in the low 100s. We soon found fish on what we read as a long uplift at 80 feet with a drop-off on either side. The temperature was an ideal 54 degrees. "But they may have started their spawning fast and not be feeding," Lievense warned. We doubled after trolling a quarter of a mile and doubled again on the figure-eight we made back through the school the graph showed. A down weight hung up on a large rock, and we backed up to free it. We went on to limit out on Chinook for each of us, with one laker for Lievense and a brown I picked up on the shore tack to the launch ramp.

In this successful troll, we used the thermometer to get out of hot water! Had we followed our minds we'd probably have stuck with the river-mouth habitat, because we'd have *known* that the fish were assembled in onshore river-current influence. But our thermometers checked by graph usage took us to the correct colder water. In the early-spring trolling described in Chapter 4 we used the thermometer to avoid cold water.

Throughout this work we've tried to understand water physics so we can know where to put our thermometer. A nurse puts a hand on the patient's brow, notes the color of the skin, and makes an educated guess about the patient's temperature. The doctor looks at the chart or takes the thermometer from the nurse. The doctor also looks at the patient, but wants an exact check on personal observations. In midsummer, Don Torba, running the *NBC I,* and Jim Hanson, running the *NBC IV,* went out of New Buffalo to find deep water because they had looked at the lake and they "knew" the Chinook would be down deep. Their host customer had said, "God, I'd like to catch one of them big Chinook in July!" When they reached 225-foot depth, Torba hit the button to lower the Riviera Temptroll. As the pulley gears hummed, he looked away from the counter and saw enormous Chinook swimming with their dorsal fins out of the water. Hanson, about half a mile to the west, called on the radio, "Great Scot! The Chinook are walking on the water!" The surface temperature was 54 degrees! Temperature habitat is where you find it; wind and rain had cooled the surface. Torba and Hanson fished long lines (80 to 100 feet) behind shallow-set down weights. "We could have taken them with a fly rod!" Torba said. They took thirty-eight fish between crew and customers on the two boats. One lake trout weighed 20 pounds, one Chinook 26. The also took coho, lakers, and steelhead. One Chinook took two hours and ten minutes to land. Torba thought it would weigh over 30 pounds; actual weight was 20 pounds. It didn't leap. The line came up several times, but the fish didn't come to the surface until ready for the net.

A cold, fickle spring at New Buffalo illustrates the fact that the thermometer is the prime tool in the trolling trinity. In April we had cold, dry weather; in May, cold, wet weather. There were thunderstorms and high winds nearly every day. One thunderstorm spawned a tornado that kicked up sand on the New Buffalo beach. Hail nicked the paint on Torba's Walker downriggers. Charter after charter had to be canceled because of high winds and waves. When they could work, Torba and Hanson entertained their customers by limiting out on Chinook, coho, and lakers while trolling parallel to shore or by finding temperature pockets where they lay. After bringing their charters to the dock and filleting the fish, Torba and Hanson would troll in *NBC I* with the Riviera Temptroll down and the Lowrance surface gauges switched on.

"We've got one reliable alley parallel to shore with downriggers almost dragging on the beach where we usually get openers," Torba said when I stopped by on my way to Chicago. "The rest we get wherever they are. The wind and the storms just scatter the temperatures all to hell. Nowhere the same reading twice!"

While I was in Chicago, we had three days of sunshine. At Oselka's Snug Harbor, Torba came to the dock with three customers and three limits. "We trolled since 7:00 a.m. to get them, but the water temperature near shore is 58 degrees," Torba said.

"Stay tomorrow," Torba invited. "I've got an open day, and I think we're about due for some easy trolling. There hasn't been a thermocline yet this year!"

That night we had another lightning spectacular, and north winds had the gale-warning flag standing straight out at dawn. Torba's cap blew over the *NBC I* and into the water. "This will disperse all the fish and all the customers," he said.

Two days later the winds steadied and I drove back to New Buffalo. "The fish are still scattered," Torba said, "but I think we can find them now."

The sun had come out on the previous afternoon; the night had been warm. Surface temperature on the Lowrance gauge beside Torba's fuel gauge showed 50 degrees when we went out at 9:00 a.m. By noon the temperature near shore had risen 8 degrees. We had trolled parallel to the shore, then straight out to sea for 2 miles, then zigzagged our way back to the harbor mouth. In many places we'd found favorable temperature habitat for all five Great Lakes sporting species, but the graph showed no fish and the lures trolling behind the down weights didn't find any the graph couldn't see.

"Still dispersed," Torba said.

"They've got to be someplace," I said.

"Probably in the lake," Torba said.

Both of us looked 360 degrees at a trackless million acres of water. We docked and had a leisurely lunch. While we ate, the leaves on an oak in the parking lot began to stir. "An offshore wind is starting up," Torba said. While we trolled the afternoon away, the wind continued strong from the southeast. The warm water near shore was being pushed out to sea. "The cold water near shore will be coming up," Torba said. I knew that there'd be an onshore underwater current—a kind of upwelling.

That afternoon we found a thermal pocket over a reef that Torba knew about. "It's not on the charts," he said. We took two lakers, both small. Then, after trolling two miles to sea, straight away on a 280-degree course we had a double pop-up—one Chinook, one coho. The surface water had been 60 degrees, Torba had noted. The Riviera Temptroll from which the Chinook I was fighting had released was trolling in 51-degree water at 35 feet. Torba got the statistics while fighting the coho and before hitting the up buttons on the Walkers and the Riviera.

"Hell, I didn't see fish on the graph," he said after we'd netted the fish. He went back to look at the graph paper spewing onto the cabin floor. The fish were there—black fingernail marks on waxy paper. It was nearly dusk. Torba tore the graph paper out to carry it away from the shadow of the cabin hard-top.

"I wish we'd thrown out a buoy," he said. There was a rock pile graphed on the bottom near where the fish marks showed over 160-foot depth. We trolled back, trying to locate the bottom mark. No more fish showed on the graph. Near the spot where the fish took we had 60 degrees for about 10-foot depth, 53 degrees at 20 feet, then 51 at 35. Another pop-up interrupted us, but I felt slack when I grabbed the pole.

"It's getting dark," the captain said. "This'll be our starting point tomorrow." He put the boat on a 100-degree course and noted our starting time on a piece of scrap paper. In eighty minutes we had the Union Pier tower lights in sight, and Torba put the helm over for the New Buffalo harbor.

The Trolling Trinity

In the morning we reset our course. The winds were calm, the lake flat. "This is where we were yesterday," Torba said, throttling down. There were fish markings on the graph between 48 feet and 70 feet—a concentration. We set two starboard downriggers at 54 feet and two port riggers at 48 feet. The surface temperature was 65 degrees; the temperature at 48 feet was 60 degrees, at 53 feet 53 degrees. We were over 100-foot depth. Both of the starboard riggers popped up immediately, and we boated two small steelhead. The port downriggers said nothing to us.

"Do you know what we've got?" Torba said.

"Good fishing at 53 feet?" I said. The last fish had jumped out of the cooler. I cornered him in a loop of rope.

"But why?" Torba asked.

"Right temperature?"

"Let me show you some magic," Torba said. He put the Riviera Temptroll down 53 feet. The temperature read 53 degrees. He raised the sensor to 48 feet and got 60 degrees. At 40 feet the temperature was 62 degrees. At 70 feet, 45 degrees.

"The graph's marking fish both above and below the 62-foot mark," Torba said. "I'll bet at 65 feet they're lake trout."

He put Thin Devles on the lines and set the starboard riggers for 65 feet. In 1,000 yards they both produced lakers.

"Now do you know what we've got?" Torba asked.

"The real El Dorado?" I asked.

"A fisherman's thermocline," Torba said. "The first of this year!"

It was a magic day. We limited out on all species except browns. The browns had not yet joined the party in the thermocline.

The trolling trinity is invincible from bottom to top, but, like all trinitarian formulations, may require ancient tools. An example is lake trout among the crevices. Sonar doesn't show fish between the cracks of rocky bottoms, and down weights do not pause over crevices to flip lures into them, but if the graph shows lakers above the cracks, and if the thermometer shows that the habitat is right, it may be best to check between the rocks.

In fall (about mid-October through mid-November), lake trout come out of summer's deep water to spawn on shallow shoals. The term "shallow" is relative. They may spawn on rockpiles under 20 feet of water or under 45 feet. (When trolling for spawning lake trout, one may fish the bottom over fairly deep water or over extremely shallow water.) An example is a rockpile northwest of New Buffalo harbor under 45 feet that drops off at both lakeward and shoreward sides to 60 feet. I went there with Don Torba and Jim Hanson aboard *NBC I* on November 3. Bob Bonasch, an *Ohio Outdoor Journal* columnist, came along to catch a lake trout feature.

As we arrived the sun, rising from the shore, created odd shadows. It was light on the water, dark on the shore. Cottages and trees loomed dark side toward us. "We've got bottom," Torba said, looking at his Vexilar. It showed a strong signal returning from a jumble of rocks—ideal spawning habitat. The school of trolling boats, including the *Bud-R-Ru,* the *R. W. Scott,* and the *Beetle Bailey,* showed us that fish had been present. The temperature was right. We anticipated easy trolling. But after trolling our down weights just over the rocks, and sometimes into them (we had a double on rocks!), we saw no fish. Moreover, the fleet left the rockpile. "Boats have spooked the spawners back to deep water," Torba said.

"Yeah, but there may be fish in the cracks that we aren't graphing," Hanson said.

"But I'm not pounding any wire into cracks in the sidewalk!" Torba said. He turned the wheel to circle the deeper water around the rockpile while Hanson and I lowered down weights and fishing lines to 60 feet. Down there, the thermometer told us, the water temperature was optimum—51 degrees. The graph showed fish—most of them oriented to boulders, but a few suspended. None took. Forty-five minutes later after several figure-eights out to sea and back across the rockpile with many ups and downs of the electric downriggers, we still had nothing. "Fish are fasting," Torba said, reminding us that during spawning the mature lake trout may have sex on their minds instead of food.

"What was that about cracks in the sidewalk?" Hanson said.

We went back to the rockpile, rigged our down weights to bang rocks, and added an instrument of torture—the wire pounder. It's a stiff rod rigged with Sea Strand metal wire and a 1-pound ball for bouncing into the crevices. Four feet from the ball Torba tied a Troll Devle with a single Siwash hook. He handed the rig to me. I let the weight to the bottom, sat down, put the rod handle under my right calf, the rod base under the reel over my left leg, and my hand halfway up on the rod. In this position I had easy leverage for the constant up-and-down bottom-feeling "pumping" and good feel for spaces between rocks.

During the first forty-five minutes of our troll, we didn't graph any fish. "Still spooked!" Hanson said. But I took two lakers each weighing over 10 pounds from the cracks. The boats didn't come back, and lakers began showing on our graphs, so the downriggers started doing their job. They were rigged with hammered Sutton Silver spoons, size 88H. While I was taking one limit on wire, Torba, Hanson, and Bonasch took three limits. Downrigger-controlled weights produced a more effective troll (by three to one) than pounded wire, but if the fish had not come back onto spawning beds—if the fleet had returned to spook them, or sunlight had risen to a harsh angle—the wire should have "kept the skunk out of the box."

Because so many variables act to change water temperature habitat, continued probing with sonar and thermometer is necessary in all waters no matter how well known. But in some water bodies, a knowledge of the fishery can save down-weight raising and lowering, sonar echoing, and thermometer probing. Thunder Bay on Lake Huron at Alepena, Michigan, is an example. The bay has the best brown trout fishing in the Great Lakes region and some outer bay lake trout fishing. Indian nets have removed some of the fish.

Charter Captain Ed Retherford, a local schoolteacher, knows the fishery. "In the early days we dragged our thermometer around a lot trying to see the sensor on our graphs," he joked when I joined him for trolling in the last part of July 1978. A prevailing westerly wind usually cools Thunder Bay by pushing the warm surface water out. If the wind shifts to onshore (from the southeast), it may pile up warm water from Lake Huron and make the browns sluggish. In August this usually happens at least a few times. Retherford begins trolling in late April and continues through early November. The best fishing occurs in April and May, with good fishing in July, late August, and the fall. In June, alewife may come in and the browns may not take lures well. "In the last part of July or the first part of August the browns migrate from the Sulphur Island area to the North Shore of Thunder Bay," Retherford says. He thinks they may be following an alewife migration.

I arrived during the early part of the alewife migration, and just after a blow from the southeast. It had been a hot day, and Retherford was praying for rain so the bay waters would cool. His prayers were not answered. "We'll start out at dawn and take a few browns—at least—before the warming sun makes them drowsy," he said. We concentrated trolling on the northward part of the U-shaped summer trolling pattern. The down weights were set to troll about 5 feet off bottom at depths ranging from 40 feet on the downrigger counter at the easterly end of the loop we made along the North Point peninsula to 20 feet at the westerly end. The water temperature was 67 degrees—5 degrees above the usual active range. The graph showed plenty of fish.

I was pleased with two limits of silver football-shaped fish by 9:00 a.m., but Retherford grumbled about high water temperature and the alewife. "Took us twice as long as it should have," he said. As the sun rose we headed for the bell buoy marking the course from the Thunder Bay River mouth to the Lake Huron navigation lane. The depth when moving south from North Point to and beyond the buoy falls to 26, 46, 72, 90, and 109 feet. At 109 feet with 109 feet of downrigger cable down, we took our first laker. We figure-eighted the area for two more hours and took two more lakers, 6 pounds and 12 pounds. The water temperature was 49 degrees at 100 feet.

In this example we took browns that were overfed in water that was too warm, and we moved from warm brown trout water to cold lake trout water. Because Retherford had used graph, thermometer, and downrigger in Thunder Bay for many years, he knew exactly when to go where. If we'd been strangers in the bay (even strangers with a chart), we probably would not have gone out at dawn to take browns. Perhaps we wouldn't have found the lakers. So keeping a log of temperature and depth details for each troll is important. A good trolling diary is the Fishing Log by Wille Products, Brookfield, Wisconsin. It has a waterproof three-ring binder, with inventory, maintenance, and safety-check pages as well as blue fishing-diary pages. The blue pages have lined columns for lure color, depth, water depth, water temperature, species, and time of day. As each fish is caught, the column can be filled in with a few scratches of the pencil. Get the action down on paper while it's happening. That way you can leaf through the next day and know where you're at.

"The purpose of a downrigger," Tom Mandigo says in lectures sponsored by Walker, "is not fishing deep. It's controlled depth." The purpose

This 22-pound Chinook was caught as a result of skillful use of the downrigger troika (lower right)—downrigger, graph, and thermometer. (Courtesy Michigan Travel Commission.)

The Trolling Trinity   89

of a thermometer is to find the proper depth, and the purpose of a sonar is to find out whether there are fish at that preferred temperature depth. A trinity symbolized by three rings hanging together. If they do not hang together, creating one spirit, then the captain needs to go in to have *his* transducer recalibrated!

9
Trolling Tactics

Because fish like lures that move at a natural speed and with an exciting wiggle, trolling speed is important. I was listening to radio calls as Don Torba and I approached a school of coho out of New Buffalo, Michigan. Two boat captains reported running both dodger-fly and dodger-plug combinations. One was taking fish on dodger-flies but nothing on dodger-plugs. The other was taking fish on dodger-plugs but nothing on dodger-flies. We took fish on both. Why did the coho like both for us? Because Torba slowed his trolling speed with the aid of a Grizzly trolling indicator after he switched from flies to plugs on the dodgers. The other two boats were probably running slow and fast baits together—a fatal mistake when trolling. Although, theoretically, a Flatfish could be run on one line and a Northport Nailer on the other, probably only one lure would be taking fish. The boat couldn't troll at a speed that would satisfy the Flatfish's slow speed, and the Nailer's fast speed. J-Plugs can be run at a variety of speeds. Some small spoons are a slow-movement lure and must be run at slow speed. At high speed they may turn over and over in the water. So trolling speed is a critical factor in triggering strikes.

Troll your belt buckle on the bedroom rug for your cat. At fast speed the cat loses interest. At a very slow speed the cat may follow without pouncing. Vary that speed slightly or put a wiggle into the belt and the cat will pounce. Fish also react this way.

Trolling Tactics 91

A double rope running over pulleys at top and bottom of outrigger pole takes the line away from the boat so the hull won't spook fish. (Courtesy Michigan Travel Commission.)

Fishermen have a tendency to remain oriented to their boat speed even after the lines are set. But the fish aren't watching the RPM gauge. They're looking at the lure, and when we present a lure by trolling we're presenting speed, wiggle, size, and pattern, in that order of importance. If a lure's traveling too fast, the fish will be spooked or they may not be able to keep up and take at the pace they prefer. Moreover, each lure has its own built-in speed. Even if each lure were rated by RPM, we still wouldn't know what the fish is seeing because the RPM on the gauge are not the real pulling speed of the boat. An engine turning at 10 RPM in free water is moving a boat faster than an engine turning at 10 RPM in a boat bucking current, wind, or waves.

Many boats are overpowered. Engines for downrigging should be chosen with trolling speeds in mind first and running speed second. It's more important to troll at a fish-getting speed than to race to the fishing spot. If a boat is overpowered, there are two ways of slowing it down: Drag a sea anchor or install a trolling brake. (Usually changing the prop will not help.) Trolling brakes are toilet-seat–shaped, spring-loaded plates that can be lowered or raised behind the prop. Even if we take each lure and hold it over the side and fiddle with the throttle until the lure hits its best wiggle, then note down the RPM we'll still have variances in accord with wind, wave, and current. To get the fish's point of view toward a lure we need a separate indicator that registers pulling-through-the-water speed—a trolling indicator. Grizzly Tackle makes one that many captains have used. Like other indicators, it uses a lead weight, cable, and spring-loaded needle. Unfortunately, lures don't come stamped with Grizzly Tackle indicator speeds. If they did, our problem would be solved. Really, each lure has to be held over the side till it reaches its optimum wiggle, then the indicator's calibration has to be noted for that lure. If a headwind comes up, increase speed to put the indicator on the right mark; if heading downwind, throttle down to keep the indicator on the mark.

The major gain from installing a trolling-speed meter is that the captain is in touch with an object that's being trolled, like the lures, and is calibrating the rate of troll, unlike the lures. But the captain has to relate the calibration of his particular meter to the way each lure works in the water. This is another very strong reason for running lures that are compatible with each other. And it's an extremely strong reason for spending time getting to know each lure one uses.

The rage right now for trolling-speed meters is sailboat speedometers or knot meters. These are small paddlewheels that become alternators. Tiny magnets in the paddlewheel pass a solid piece of metal and generate a current, which activates a dial. The reading is accurate even for very slow speeds, and it's a report of the water passing through the paddlewheel, not the turning of the driveshaft. Moreover, the paddlewheels are instantly reponsive to the slam of a wave on the bow, the rise of a gust upon the windshield. But this accuracy doesn't excuse the captain from the time and labor of calibrating each lure or, at least, each family of lures with the instrument.

There are a number of sailboat speedometers on the market. Captain Al Tyrrell uses an EMS U25K, which is listed in the Goldberg catalog. Others include the Bristol, made in New Bedford, Massachusetts, and the VDO, made in Germany. They should not be mounted near transom or engine turbulence, and the instruments with 0- to 12-knot scales are best. Bruce DeShano uses an SR Mariner Model KT 6 knot meter. It's designed for power boats (some sailboat speedometers do not register above 10 knots). The chart in Figure 20 gives DeShano's trolling speeds with the KT6.

A captain must exercise considerable skill backed up with experience to know the trolling speed of all the lures he has on board, the way his own boat trolls through wind and wave, and which lures team well together. Careful records in the fishing log and experience with a trolling indicator he likes will help him.

	Knot Meter Speeds for Lures
J-Plug	2 knots
Fire Plug	¾ to 1½ knots
Flutter Spoons	dead slow to 2½ knots
Northport Nailers	dead slow to 4 knots
Fishback	2 knots
Loco	2 knots
Clatter Tad	¾ to 1½ knots
Krocodile	to 4 knots

Figure 20. *These speeds are for the SR Mariner KT6 on Captain DeShano's Sport-Craft C-Eagle.*

The captain also considers his trolling swath—the width of water he can cover with the number of rods it's legal for him to set. He will create trolling patterns that make his lures work over the habitat he sees on his sonar. For example, if a sharply dropping reef is located, the captain may want to lengthen the line from down weight to bait and troll across the top of the ridge, then lower the weight progressively to make the lure travel downhill. Another method of covering a drop-off is to troll along the deep side in a zigzag pattern. The lure then travels uphill until depth is shallow, then downhill until depth is deeper than a fish might rise from. A figure-eight trolling pattern is used in many situations. A tight figure-eight will "cause the lures to change speed and to rise and fall just as a baitfish does when evading its predator," James Kammeraad says. Several figure-eights one on top of the other ensure that graphed fish that do not respond are completely covered with presenting lures. The captain will remember that on sonar, fish are frequently at shallower depth than the gauge indicates.

The depth at which four downriggers should be run is also an important consideration. One rule of thumb is one rig somewhat under graphed fish, one rig somewhat above, and two rigs right on. Some captains set by temperature. Captain Art Dittmar, writing in *The Michigan Steelheaders' Guide to Great Lakes Sport Fishing*, explains a method he uses when fishing for lakers off Michigan's Manistee River. "Using my temperature gauge, I find the 49- to 51-degree water depth. I like to run my deepest line at 49-degree level and my top line at 51 degrees. I stagger my other two downriggers between these two if possible." With this method, Dittmar spans the species' preference range. Water temperatures may make this possible for other species where you troll.

Of course all sets must take into consideration the problem of fouling lines on turns. Dittmar, who runs port and starboard side riggers, usually does this by running the port side rigger at 40 feet, the starboard side rigger at 35 feet, the starboard stern downrigger at 50 feet, and the port stern downrigger at 45 feet. This pattern, which keeps the side riggers at shallower depth than the stern downriggers, prevents tangling at turns.

Species vary a great deal on the distance behind the down weights they'll take. Norm Newman, professional fisherman for Riviera, gives line distances behind the downrigger for saltwater species in Figure 23 (in Chapter 13). The rule of thumb is that the shallower one fishes, the longer the line; the deeper, the shorter. When fishing shallow one should troll slowly, Newman says, because fish at the surface swim more slowly than they do in deep water. Don Christenson, a charter captain in Newport,

It is best to plan trolling tactics from a clean deck. Note storage doors below gunwale, lures stored in see-through boxes, easy-access plug-ins, two rod holders for stacking at each downrigger.

Oregon, says that most of his fish are caught on short lines, "1, 2, 3, or 6 feet from the boat."

When your graph is painting fish on the bottom, a good way to hit them on the head is to take the engine out of gear. The lure will flutter downward. This is also a good way to catch down weights in cracks. Another way is to turn tightly to make the inside lures move downward. Lake trout or bass that ignore a lure presented at the graphed depth may be enticed by a line-tripping maneuver. Pop the line to allow the lure to flutter to surface. The laker may chase the lure upward and nail it near the top. Remember that changing trolling speeds may induce a strike.

Because dodger and flasher action depend on trolling speed, I will discuss them in this chapter. Both dodgers and flashers create flashes of light, but each has a different action. Flashers rotate. Dodgers wobble and swing from side to side. Start a dodger at slow speed and increase speed until the wobbling, side-to-side motion is regular, with a snappy beat. Start a flasher in the same way. As speed increases it will move from side to side, then begin revolving. Keep the throttle set right on revolving or give it a light tap. This is the correct trolling speed.

In the state of Washington, at least, dodgers preceded flashers. The pendulum movement or side-to-side movement was the first method used to reflect light to attract fish. Obviously, this motion reflected light toward the surface and the bottom, but not to either side unless the dodger was tilted by wave action. An old-timer in Port Angeles, Al McKnight, took some large dodgers and experimented with multiple bends until he got one to rotate in a circle as he trolled it. He called it a rotating flasher, and eventually it was marketed under the name Abe & Al. Luhr Jensen still makes the flasher in sizes 6, 8, 10, 1, and 2. I prefer Kelly green, fire, and chartreuse for hunting fish in open water. The white is best in murky waters such as river mouths in the fall.

Dodgers and flashers are possibly heard or felt by the fish first, then seen. The pulsating movement of a working dodger may bring a fish close enough to see the flashes of light. That may entice the fish even closer.

Dodgers and flashers have a head end and a tail end. Usually, the tail has both a swivel and an added double eyelet made by twisting wire. This rear eyelet is an open twist, so a loop can be turned down the corkscrew into the eyelet. That's for the trailing bait, fly, or lure. When rigging, begin by following the manufacturer's recommendations on leader length from sinker to dodger and from dodger to lure. These are usually particularly accurate for flies and for frozen bait, but may not be totally accurate for the range of plugs that can be run behind dodgers. You may want to lengthen the leader out until the plug regains its own action independent of the dodger's beating.

Captain Bernie Halverson, in a feature printed in *The Michigan Steelheader,* "Suggestions on Dodgers," says that he removes treble hooks from plugs to be run behind dodgers and replaces them with a Siwash hook mounted point up. "This method seems to stand the severe strain a fighting fish can impose while jerking or jumping against the close-by weight and momentum of a dodger," he says.

Dodgers and flashers are built with many bends and curves. An Abe &

Al flasher has a long S curve and two bends at each end. A Martin Tackle and Manufacturing Company superflasher achieves its S shape with six bends. Each bend or curve has a relationship to the other bends or curves. They produce a series of planes. So it's possible to knock everything out of alignment by dropping a down weight on them. Martin sends a template with each flasher so they can be kept in alignment. They're supposed to have a head angle of 12 degrees and a tail angle of 16 degrees. To increase the action of a dodger or flasher, increase the bend at the lure end. To reduce action, increase the bend at the rod end.

Charter Captain John Lievense, who's run several different boats, finds that different manufacturers' dodgers fit the trolling speed of different boats. In one boat he found that Les Davis flashers, made of thin-gauge metal, worked best. In another boat, he found that Luhr Jensen and Martin Tackle flashers worked best. He says that it's up to the captain to experiment until he finds trolling speeds that synch well with dodgers and flashers.

Cowbells are strings of blades that can be trolled behind down weights to excite fish to take a following lure. Like dodgers and flashers, they excite fish by flashing light, and making a sonic beat. It's confusing to consider them because of the bewildering number of names their inventors have contributed. To select the "bells" that are best for your water, it's wise to learn them by blade rather than by brand name. Willow leaf and Colorado blades are shapes that most fishermen know. Two catalogs picture other blade shapes. Luhr Jensen shows exact size and pattern for Ford Fender (originally cut by the firm's founder from his Model T headlights), Beer Can, Mounti, Diamond, Doc Shelton, Main Train, Bear Valley, and Baby Gang. Dave Davis advertises Standard, Giant, and Baby Cowbells, Jack-O-Diamonds, Slim Jim, Odd Ball, Canadian Flash, and bolo blades. That firm also sells strings of willow leaves dressed with Scalelite. Fishermen get the impression that all cowbells do the same thing. What do the fish think? Probably an answer to this question would bring a captain a great many fish. They attract fish with sound and light and can be obtained in many colors and painted. Thus they can be used with color-depth penetration (see Chapter 10) in mind. We should be able to put all these variables together, experiment, and catch more fish.

Remember that releases can be attached behind dodgers, flashers, and cowbells. Many of the releases on the market will work well when a fish strikes, but not all of them will release on an upward pull from the fisherman. The rig trailing at a distance from the stability of the down weight may lift upward and tangle.

Trolling Tactics 97

Putting the outriggers down solves the problem of spooking fish with the boat hull and may increase the motion of flat-line lures. Outriggers have releases that the fish pop when they strike. Because the outriggers rise and fall with wave action, lures presented on them are surface-jigged or danced. This jigging action can be increased by adding weight. Tom Mandigo uses a wire line and lead on outriggers. A Western custom that's used on the Great Lakes is to increase the depth of jigging with a sinker release and an 8- to 16-ounce weight.

Another way of taking fish spooked by the boat is to use side surface planers. They come in pairs. Right-hand boards are cut to "water-ski" to starboard of a moving boat as the guide rope is let out. Left-hand boards go to port. A planer can be sent out as far as 200 feet. This certainly increases the trolling path.

Despite their effectiveness, many planing boards are disappointing because the fisherman has to fight the board to get the fish. (Homemade releases can be added to some of them.) Another disadvantage is that most planing boards are restricted to presenting surface lures. The invention of the Sea Skee marketed by Wille Products, Brookfield, Wisconsin, has solved these two problems. Sea Skees come with gripper-type releases—one for the board (a flag trips up when it releases) and several for the tow line. Sea Skees will also support weights up to 3 pounds, so one can fish deep from the board. Deep Sixes, Pink Ladies, or other diving devices can be run from them. The buoyancy of these boards can be adjusted by putting water in any of eight reservoirs. I find that they work well in waves up to 5 feet. Traditionally, boards have been used when sonar shows no fish at surface. Sea Skees can be used when fish are deeper. Lures that run well at all speeds are best for planers. The reason is that their speed may change from slow to fast during turns.

It's up to the captain to keep the lures all walking at a good pace and to watch for variations of motion that can create good trolling tactics. The best tactics are conceived in the field in reaction to actual events. This was illustrated the year Andy Pelt, executive director of the Michigan Steelhead and Salmon Fisherman's Association, was aboard the Michigan City Tournament winning boat with Mike Lummis, Vern Sherrod, and Tom Mandigo. Lakers were being painted on their graph, but for half an hour they trolled with no hits. Changes of lures and lure combinations didn't improve the score. So the next step was to vary trolling speeds and directions. They were trolling a zigzag pattern and making a turn when the inside outrigger took an 11-pound laker, Pelt reports. As the team reviewed this take, they realized that the 3/16-ounce Grizzly Spooner that took the fish on the inside outrigger had settled with a fluttering action when they turned. They decided to duplicate this fluttering action on all seven rods instead of only one during turns. To control this, they lowered a hydraulic trolling plate made by Beaver-Trol during each turn. They also switched to Luhr Jensen hammered chrome and brass Flutter Spoons. This on-the-spot trolling tactic based on trolling speed and the variation of that speed gave the team a tournament win with five coho, five lake trout, and one steelhead.

10
Choosing the Right Lures

I ask myself the four questions answered in this chapter each time I fish. I ask to be sure I've covered all the variables the fish encounter.

What spoons, plugs, jigs, flies, and spinners have colors that lure fish to them? The fisherman tries to solve the reaction of fish to color by looking at lures lighted in the atmosphere. Fish look at lures underwater, and water, unlike atmosphere, filters color rays out by depth. Some colors penetrate a few feet, others many feet; so an understanding of color penetration will help fishermen select and paint lures.

Before we discuss color penetration, let's consider some other information about the sight of fish. Frank Brown, Jr., while a professor at the University of Illinois, worked with *bass* and learned that they see color nearly as humans do—probably as though looking through a yellow filter. Most biologists agree that fish see color. But bottomfish—skates, rays, and flounders—do not have rods in the retinas, seem to lack color perception, and react only to light intensity. Fish come to and investigate objects the same color as their food. They can be conditioned to react to a color. Fish reacting in aquarium experiments seem to prefer the warm colors: red, orange, and yellow, in that order. Perhaps their eyes do function nearly like humans eyes, but their brains are not like human brains, and they see in underwater conditions that are extremely dissimilar to the conditions of human sight. So we need to think about the conditions of fish perception, and we must realize that they don't read the ads on the lure packages.

To fishermen, sunlight looks clear. Actually, it's a mixture of infrared, red, orange, yellow, green, blue, violet, and ultraviolet. From our point of view, lures are colored. But a lure reflects the colors we see and absorbs all the other colors the sun sends. Light waves can be filtered to the point of blockage by various substances including water. These factors are all

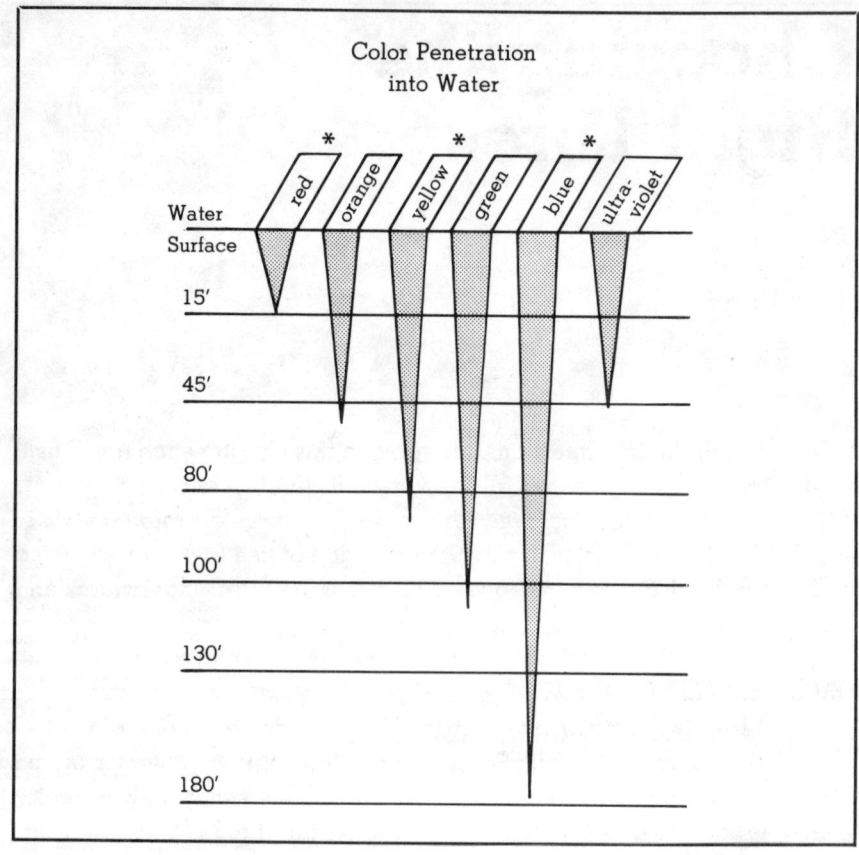

Figure 21. *The depths a color will penetrate water under ideal conditions—high noon; clear water. Below 15 feet, the red light waves are filtered out. The orange, yellow, green, and blue waves continue to penetrate. In the zone below the penetration of blue, fish see colors as gray to black. Untraviolet rays, within a relatively shallow zone, convert fluorescent color pigments into light rays. Caution: This figure does not show the length of light waves. The asterisks indicate the three primary pigments, not the primary light colors. Fishermen carrying primary pigments in their tackle box can mix colors for painting lures the hues fish see as desirable. (Data gathered by Stan Lievense. Used by permission of the Michigan Department of National Resources Education and Information Division and the Michigan Tourism Council.)*

Choosing the Right Lures

a fisherman needs to know to understand penetration and reflection of the light that reaches lures under water. But the fishermen can become confused. Remember that Figure 21 does not show the *length* of light waves. It shows the penetration of light into a filter—water. Remember that when you paint lures, the three pigment primaries for mixing colors are red, yellow, and blue. Do not use the light primaries.

In water fish see less color as they swim deeper because water resists the penetration of the sun's light waves. In other words, as light penetrates water, colors filter out. When a color is filtered out, the light spectrum is changed. In Figure 21 we see that the loss of red at 15 feet changes the color spectrum to orange, yellow, green, and blue. (Neither fish nor fishermen see ultraviolet.) There are two reasons why water alters the spectral composition of penetrating light. First, water selectively absorbs light waves of different lengths. Second, materials carried in water (both absorbed and mixed) lower and change light transmission. Organic coloring filters out the blue end of the color spectrum. Plankton not only reduces transmission but also absorbs more short than long waves.

At 180 feet, where color no longer penetrates, fish see colored lures as gray to black. But experiments with divers show that black is not a highly visible underwater color—perhaps because of low contrast against the dark, deep-water background. Therefore, we should not immediately jump to the conclusion that all lures fished below 180 feet should be black or gray. It may be that no color change is needed below 180 feet because the fish see the lure as black and gray. On the other hand, highly contrasting grays and blacks in a range of hues might excite deep-lying fish. So better black and gray lures could, possibly, be created. If you're running lures above 180-foot depth to fish that have risen from below, a gray or black lure might work because the fish may still have a set for a dark lure.

When we say that water depth affects color penetration, we're thinking of calm water with light directly overhead. Figure 21 is drawn on that premise. The angle of the light also affects penetration. (See Figure 22.) In early morning or late afternoon, the sun's rays are at a low angle. The first color to show beneath the surface in the early morning light is blue. As blue penetrates, green appears. As blue and green penetrate, yellow reflects beneath the surface. As blue, green, and yellow penetrate, orange reflects below the surface. As blue, green, yellow, and orange penetrate, red reflects below the surface. Saying it in this long way helps to explain that we are dealing with a spectrum or range of color—a *mixture* of light waves. A mixture of paint, as the artist knows best, retains the spectrum or mixture that is natural lighting. (Realistic plugs achieving hues through a mixture of paint probably do better than those achieving hue through a thin coat.) As the sun sets, the depth of color penetration changes in reverse order. Remember to put your brain into reverse gear when applying this morning knowledge to evening fishing. In your mind's eye, put a sun rising from the east (the right) over Figure 21; then see it sinking from noon to sunset toward the west (the left). Thus from

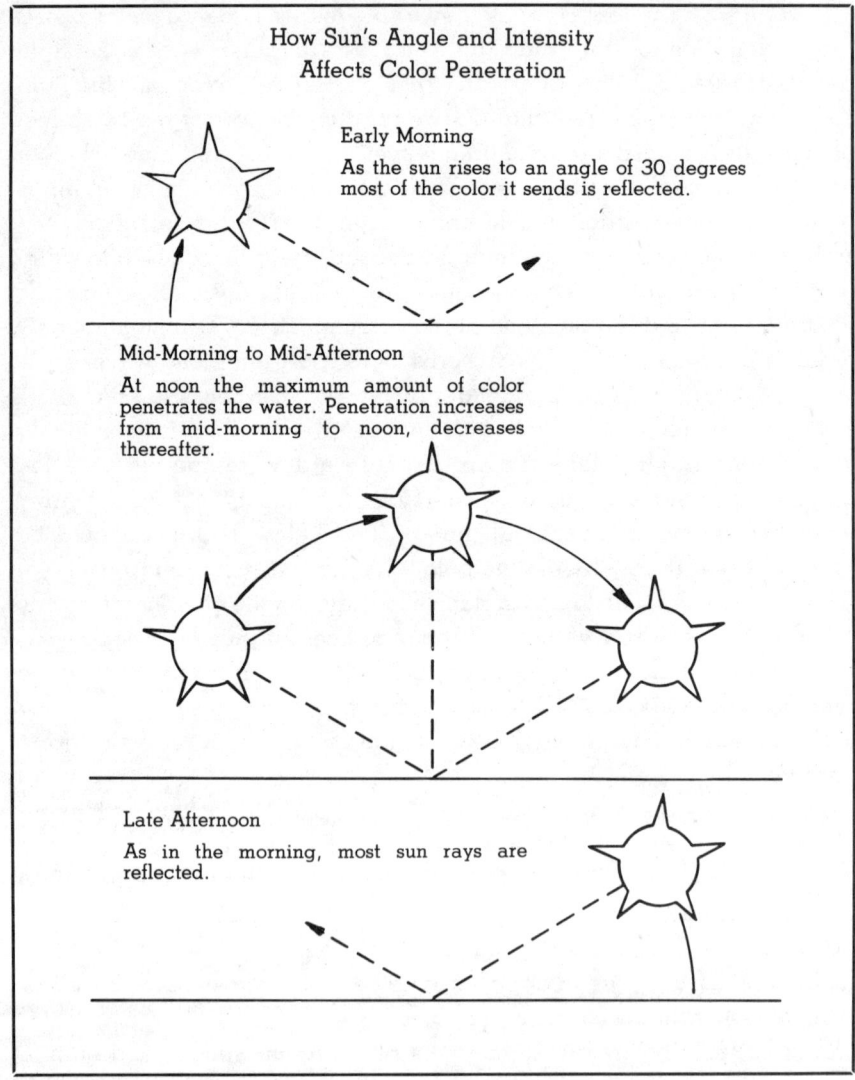

Figure 22. *Data gathered by Stan Lievense. Published by permission of the Michigan Department of National Resources Education and Information Division, and the Michigan Travel Bureau.*

morning to noon your mind puts lures in from blue lures to green lures, to yellow, to orange, to red. (Of course, color mixtures are understood.) Then from noon till darkness, you reverse the direction of thought, taking colors out from red to blue.

So far, we've been talking about direct sunlight. Diffused sky light also lights the fish's world. Light allows cover as haze increases diffused sky lighting.

Now that we've discovered that the angle of light affects penetration as well as the depth of the water, we have opened the door to many considerations. How early in the morning is blue the first color to show? How early on a calm day when the water is still? How early on a windy day when waves affect the angle of penetration? Clearly, fishing experience is needed to answer these questions.

Stan Lievense has done some of the pioneering color fishing. He's the author of *Spectrum Fishing*, published by the Best Tackle Company, and "Catching Great Lakes Salmon & Trout," published by the Michigan Department of Natural Resources. He's gathered together a number of facts about light and color that fishermen should consider. White lures gather light rays and reflect them with diffusion. Black, the absence of color or the total absorption of all light waves, gives maximum contrast. Nickel and silver reflect light rays like a mirror. Gold and brass reflect yellow rays. Blue, white, and silver lures are best for deep fishing. Ultraviolet rays cannot be seen by fish or humans, but they convert fluorescent color pigments into light rays. "Hence," Lievense says, "a fluorescent red-colored lure can be seen as a red lure deeper than ordinary during good light conditions."

Kinney, Luria, and Weitzman did research on underwater color visibility to humans. Fishermen can benefit from their controlled findings recorded at the Naval Submarine Base in Connecticut. In summary, their findings are: (1) There is considerable difference in visibility of color from water body to water body. (2) The human perception of color changes from water body to water body. (3) Fluorescent colors are seen more easily during deep diving than nonfluorescent colors. However, in extremely clean water the fluorescent energy may be lost before it reaches the human eye. (4) Red is not transmitted well in clear water; blue and green are not transmitted well in murky water. (5) Black is not a highly visible underwater color.

Kinney, Luria, and Weitzman were concerned about helping to create signs that divers and submarine pilots can see underwater. Fishermen are concerned with creating lures that fish can see. So the conclusions about color visibility that the naval researchers reached may be helpful. They were: (1) For rivers, harbors, and other turbid bodies of water, fluorescent orange is the most visible. (2) For coastal waters of mediocre clarity, fluorescent green and orange are superior. (3) For clear water, fluorescent greens and white are the best. (4) Fluorescent materials are superior to nonfluorescent materials of the same color in all water bodies.

The fact that there is considerable difference in visibility of color from water body to water body ought to encourage fishermen to do more research and to paint their own lures. The lures we buy are created for a general purpose—to work in all water. The water we fish may require a color modification.

The fact that people see color differently when in different water boggles the mind. Divers in the Thames, for example, saw blue as green, yellow as orange, and orange as red. The scientific explanation was: "In water that transmits more of the long waves than of the short, e.g., the Thames, the perceived colors change toward the longer wavelengths." Does this mean that a blue lure that's supposed to work better at 180 feet because all other colors are filtered out by that depth might be perceived by the fish as some other color? Perceived as blue, that is, at 180 feet in Lake Superior, but as some other color at 180 feet in a western impoundment? We don't know. But there is an element of order in this color confusion: The appearance of each color is almost always changed toward the ones closest to it on either side of the spectrum." This means that if the blue lure doesn't take fish sighted on the graph at 180 feet, a lure painted contrasting blue and green might work, or even better, a lure with blue-and-green stripes separated by a black stripe.

This information opens the market to the sale of nude lures. Fishermen are painting their own lures. Grizzly Tackle sells fluorescent paints, and Herter's and Hille's Angler's Supply House market unpainted lures. Many carry paint boxes.

The upside-down lure created, we understand, by Stan Lievense is related to the subject of color penetration and visibility. (Buzz Ramsey and Luhr Jensen field testers have been painting Coach Dogs upside-down for several years.) The upside-down idea arose from Lievense's thinking about camouflage. In Big Water, fish wearing what we call protective sea camouflage are green on their backs and silver on their bellies. A predator looking down on a fish sees the green back against the green depths and bottom. Because the two greens merge, the fish is not so easily seen. A predator looking up sees the silver belly merged into the light sky and surface water above. Lures painted in exact imitation of fish have the same camouflage, making it *difficult* for the fish to see them. "Fishermen have unwittingly been hiding their lures," Lievense says. The remedy: Reverse the paint. Put the green back paint on the belly and the silver belly paint on the back.

What spoons, plugs, jigs, flies, and spinners have motions that lure fish to them? How do we put an "aquatic wiggle" into a lure? Fish have a set for motion. Like a cat following a string, they'll follow the wiggle of a moving lure. What lure motions excite strikes? This is the major problem that Stan Lievense seeks to solve with his motion fly, the Stanley Streamer. When we tow a fly behind a down weight, we aren't imitating anything. If we put a screw eye in a doll's head and pulled it behind our down weight, it wouldn't look like a man swimming. A pulled fly doesn't look like a fish or an insect swimming. Placing a flange on the front of a fly makes it wiggle. A part of that wiggle is very much like the movement of an aquatic insect—but only part of the movement. If we put flanges on a doll's arms, the arms would move up and down—but only part of that movement would look like an arm swimming. So aquatic wiggles are an abstraction of the motions fish see underwater creatures making. And the range of aquatic wiggles is limited to the actions that can be achieved by an object being pulled through water by a fishing line.

Lures can be divided into families by their shape and the aquatic wiggle their shape achieves in water. This family division was summarized by Captain John Lievense, an Eppinger executive. The Bass-Oreno plug developed by South Bend, now owned by Glen Evans, is the father of a large family of plugs that share a similar shape and aquatic wiggle. This wiggle was used in early Pacific salmon trolling plugs, among them the Lucky Louie. In downrigger plugs, its representatives are Lucky Luhr, J-Plug, Canadian Plug, Witch Doctor, Spar-X, and Burke SA-Mon plug. The lessons to be learned from distinctive, individual refinements in these lures will be discussed later.

As we discuss Captain Lievense's families to gain a vision of the wiggles possible for towed "objects," remember that each member of the family may differ widely from others. And the examples under each family tree are only some of the many manufactured lures that could be cited.

The Pencil Family is a distinctively shaped set of lures represented by Rappala and Rebel minnow imitations. They work well behind down weights. Deep Diver Family members are represented by Hell Bender, Bomber, Big Dig, and Bagley's deep-diver small fry. Jointed Family representatives include Rebel's 2½-inch J-50 minnow imitation and Creek Chub's 11-inch Giant Pikie. The Surface Plug Family may include a lot of floating lures that can be lowered on down weights and trolled. But family members could be restricted to lures like Injured Minnow and Jitterbug. In the Banana Family, Lievense includes Flat Fish, Lazy Ike, Tadpolly, and Hot Shot. The Drift-Fishing Family, not to my knowledge used in downrigging, includes Woble Glow, Glo-Go, Peanuts, Okie-Drifter, and Jumping Jack. Crank Bait Family members include the Hot 'N Tot, Fat Rat, Big O, and Tennessee Shad. Thin Spoon Family members, important to downrigger fishermen because they flow with towing-generated turbulence and because they can be hand-tuned, include thin spoons from Eppinger, Luhr Jensen, Herter's, and Best Tackle. They can be finger-shaped: for slow trolling, shape like a tablespoon bent in a lazy curve; for fast trolls, straighten; for intermediate needs, take hold at each end and twist in opposite directions or make an angular S shape by bending upward near one end and downward at the opposite end. The Dinner Table Spoon Family, which originated when Julio Buel used his mother's silver for a lure, includes several DarDevles, Little Cleo, Big Doctor, Little Doctor, K-B 4, and some Marathon spoons. One Little Cleo is the same size as a Devle-Dog. They seem similar in shape, but one has a scantily clad dancing girl (Cleo) for the fish to inspect and the other has Satan's face. Tablespoon-shaped lures used by downriggers include Devle-Dog, for all salmonids; Troll Devle, often used for lake trout on wire line; Dardevlet, used by Lievense for Chinook in late fall; and the *willow* blade Klicker series that creates sonic sound. There's a final family of Non-Dinner Table Spoons. Most of these, like the tablespoon shapes, have concave-convex waterflow foils, but they may also have two other geometric shapes or foils—bend action planes and elongated streamlin-

The lure being removed from the mouth of this 4-pound bass can be returned to its hanger in the Wille Bait File. Because it's a hot lure, it's a good idea to cross-reference it for color, size, and action for future use.

ing. These include K-O Wobbler, Thin-Doctor (a two-action-in-one-lure reverse hook and snap), Andy Reeker, Krocodile, Martin Crow and Martin Fishmor, Loco, and Point Defiance. The Point Defiance is not a thin flutter spoon and can't be hand-tuned. It has a bent plane creating a definite action.

This lure family typology will help trolling captains remember what's already been lowered for fish inspection and rejection, while trying to decide what to try next. Too often we repeat our errors by giving the fish something they've already seen. A new brand name may not mean a new aquatic motion or a lure more nearly adjusted to our engine's trolling speed. A tackle box that can be easily labeled by lure family is the Bait File by Wille Products. I type family names on self-adhesive file-folder labels and stick them to the outside frame of these flip-file lure holders. A

Cut herring compared with Scalelite finish on No. 4 Point Defiance spoon. The light-shadow effect of the Scalelite seems to be quite convincing to fish.

lure family is ranked with a lure of each color in a row from right to left (i.e., from east or sunrise to west or sunset) in the order of color penetration as shown in Figure 21. Labeling the lures will make it easier to determine if another one could be substituted if the one you're using isn't catching fish. Moreover, one of the lures in the file may be tuned or painted to fit the description of the fish-getter on a buddy's line.

Thus on shipboard I turn from the compass to the Bait File and orient it to east-west, or sun-path line, so I can choose lure hue by angle of penetration. At the same time, I am imagining myself to be underwater at a temperature depth I've read off the trolling thermometer. Then as I'm kneeling before the Bait File absorbed in underwater thought, I like to look up from the ranked lures to the graph. At such times, I am kneeling in thought, and much of my thought is directed to the sun. How much light is *it* sending? How much heat has *it* given the wind to mix into the water? What lure family, what specific lure color will work?

I also carry several bottles of paint, brushes, thinner for cleaning the brushes, stick-on tape in many colors, and flashes.

What causes false releases and rod tip telegraphing? Often it's fish mouthing hooks that don't hook them. I see the fish doing this through polarized lenses when using exciter fishing methods to take fish on flies in rivers. Charlie White's Saltaire-sponsored underwater movies show that salmon do the same thing to trolled lures. We have more strikes than we know about because fish can use their gills, tongues, and jaws in unison to spit out lures. The remedy is to sharpen all hooks. Some charter captains have the first mate file hooks while running to trolling grounds. Don't sharpen by filing round! Sharpen left side and right side, Lefty Kreh style, to create a triangular shape at hook point.

If your rod tip is telegraphing misses, you may have chosen a lure that's nearly right. The fish that mouthed the lure was attracted to it! Try a size smaller or larger.

What do fish "hear" that attracts them? What vibrations repel them? The ears of many species are attached to their bladders, which act as resonators. Furthermore, their lateral lines are important receptors for underwater vibrations. I think maybe fish triangulate vibrations by using both their ears and their lateral lines. Possibly all the sonic sounds created by sonic lures are sensed by both the lateral line and the ear. Sonic lures used by downrigger captains include Sculpin Sounder, Clatter Tadpolly, Marek's, L-Lures, and Killer Diller. All of them combine aquatic action, color, and sound. Whether the addition of the sound is positive or negative can't be clear until we hang some microphones into fish tanks and learn more about which vibrations attract fish. Fish hear all kinds of sounds from trolling boats. Vibrations are sent by the hull, the down cables, the weights, the lines, the hooks, and the snaps and swivels. Some of these repel; some attract. Furthermore, some fish may be responding to the sighted turbulence caused by the "noise maker." How do we rule out these contradictory variables? Perhaps by fishing a Tadpolly with a Clatter Tadpolly at the same depth. These two lures, Heddon's John Marsman reports, are the same size and have the same aquatic wiggle. Unfortunately, their paint patterns differ. But Marsman is sending me Tads and Clatter Tads with identical paint patterns NPC and FYR. They'll be sent down behind down weights for what Bernie Halverson calls "fish inspection and selection." If fished behind down weights of identical size and shape, at the same depth, for many hours and in many different habitats, these teamed lures may tell us whether fish prefer to hear or see the Tadpolly.

11
Fighting Fish with Rod and Reel

Rodmakers were puzzled when downrigger inventors began rigging rods down. The J-shaped torque of the rod tip toward the release took word-of-mouth precedence over the speed of the bend. In the past, the speed with which the rod tip bent and the amount of that bend related directly to the timing of casts. But downriggers don't cast when they set their rods, and the way rods torque down seemed, at first, more important than the way they cast. Power, the amount of weight a rod is built to cast, was another traditional asset built into rods that didn't seem totally relevant to the way downriggers set their lines. Length was another specification that took on new meaning. In the past, the distance of the cast, the weight to be cast, the height of the caster, and the terrain over which he cast were considerations. Now the distance from the rod holder to the planed-out down weight, the amount of outboard engine width, the swimming platform width, and the length of the downrigger boom became considerations. Confusion also arose over trolling-rod traditions. Many of them, particularly those called boat rods, were of stiff action and heavy butt, with large wooden handles and with the guides mounted on the spline of the rod. But downriggers found that the wooden handles wouldn't fit into rod holders, that the boat-rod actions were too heavy, and that they needed the guides mounted on the side opposite the spline. Another worry was whether or not torquing the rod fatigued the tip.

Out of this ferment there arose, as usual, a too-easy answer. Rods were

Chinook (left) and coho with the casting reel that took them from Lake Michigan. The scalloped control between handle and reel is the star drag; the free-spool lever is at the top. (Courtesy Michigan Travel Commission.)

to have a flyrod tip action and a heavy butt. Many were rushed onto the market under this advertising slogan. The well-made ones had fast-action tips with the action extending far into the butt. These endured. Those not so well made had a tip action that stopped at or near the joining of front and butt. This made a fulcrum that provided leverage that wore the hook out of fish's mouths and created a breaking point that sometimes relieved the owner of the burden of using the rod. But there were well-crafted flexible-tip stiff-butt rods on the market that did not break and handled fish well. I found one among my steelhead rods. It's a Shakespeare Kwik Taper Wonderod, No. A 622, for spinning, and I still use it. It has most of its action in the tip 23 inches, but this action travels well into the butt. It torques well, making a decent J shape, and dampens fairly well, although some tip vibrations do occur at pop-up. The handle is a little short for downrigger rod holders, but fits in, and the cork clearly conducts fish action to the hands. Shakespeare designers didn't build the rod for downrigging. I bought it for steelheading in small Upper Peninsula streams. But it worked, so there was something for the downrigger in the Shakespeare cupboard and in many other rod companies' lines.

Gradually I built up a list of specifications for downrigger rods. The ideal length is 8 feet 3 inches. The rod tip should extend out over the water to a point above the release. The thickness of the gunwale, the position of the rod holder, and the length of the downrigger boom are all considerations in establishing this length. Some 7-foot rods work well; in some instances, longer rods are needed. But a rod tip that doesn't extend to a point above the release doesn't J well and may build a fulcrum that will slip line through releases. What is meant by J'ing? That's the shape rods make when they're torqued (tightened down by turning the reel handle) so the tip will help release the line and hook the fish by popping up when the fish pulls the line from the release. Some rod builders see a C shape, but it's really better described as a J. What is meant by "build a fulcrum that will slip line through releases"? If the rod tip distance is short of the release, the line will take up a fulcrum on one of the guides and pull so hard against the workings of the release in the water that it will slip, and slip within the release. And the fisherman will torque and retorque until all of the line has slipped through the release and the lure is riding against it. This can happen on light settings with all kinds of releases, but particularly happens with button releases.

Rods should torque to a light drag setting. In other words, the tip action should be light enough to allow it to be tightened into a J shape without tightening the drag. Some stiff rods put so much tension on the line when they're J'd that line pays off the drag. The remedy is to set the drag up beyond a point allowable for the strike of a heavy fish. Some rods will J on a reasonable drag setting if the line is "milked." Milking is pulling the line toward the reel with the fingers of one hand on the line between the first guide and the reel. Take up by turning the reel handle with the other hand. But milking will only put the last curve into the J. Of course, the relationship between drag setting and J'ing is relative. When ocean fishing for species over 100 pounds, the proper rod is too stiff to be J'd. When fishing the Inside Passage for 60-pound Chinook, a stiff graphite rod may be used that can only be partially J'd on a reasonable drag setting.

One of the puzzles of downrigger rod building that's sorted itself out is the relationship of J'ing to tip action. We've discovered that the J length for nearly all rods is the same as the action bend. For example, a Fenwick-Woodstream FS83 torques 33 inches of the tip, and when held in the action-determining position bends 33 inches of tip. (When I say "action-determining position," I'm thinking of Dale Clemens' definition in his book, *Fiberglass Rod Making,* of extra-fast, fast, medium, and slow action.) This fact answers a number of rod builders' questions. Downrigger rods can be made according to the speed of the casting bend and with comparable power. The tip will not fatigue from torquing any more than any casting rod fatigues at the action bending point.

Downrigger rods should conduct fish action as well as a drift rod conducts the ticking of a lead weight over gravel. I call this "conductivity."

Steelheaders call it "drift sensitivity." I want to use fairly light line and to be able to feel the muscles of my fish when I make my initial high-sweeping pickup from the rod holder.

The handles should be long, so the reel is well above the lips of the rod holder. About 14 inches of handle below the reel is a good distance. There are two reasons for this. First, the handle must mate well into the rod holder or it will fly out when the boat bounces over the waves. Second, the reel and reel handle should be high enough to clear other gear. The handles should be cork with some cork above the reel, so the hands will receive conductivity and be comfortable while fighting the fish. Nylon foam and other synthetic materials reduce conductivity.

Because the guides on a downrigger rod must be closer together, more are needed. When an 8-foot, 3-inch rod is resting upright in the holder, three guides are enough to distribute the line evenly from guide to guide. But when that rod is J'd the stretched line makes a shortcut from guide to guide and rubs on the rod curving beneath the guides. "Abrasion on the guides and the rod ruins lines," Dick Swan, maker of Swan light lining rods, points out. So downrigger rods should have more guides correctly spaced over the J'ing area.

As we've worked this specification up, we've developed several reasons for rejecting the old stiff-butt flyrod-tip spec. The action of a downrigger rod should distribute evenly from the tip into the fisherman's hand. Conduction, playing fish on "light" line, and J'ing all demand well-crafted rods. A flexible tip action that halts within a stiff butt doesn't permit sufficient extension of the senses into water.

If you move from boat to boat across two regions, as I do, you'll find rods of many specifications torqued to down-weighted releases. Furthermore, downrigger rods have come from many rod company cupboards. This means, as Dale Clemens has pointed out to me, that there's a hodgepodge of rods in use. They can all be made to do the job. Nevertheless, I feel that a downrigger-styled rod can evolve from the specifications I suggest. To summarize, a downrigger rod should be at least 8 feet 3 inches long, should torque to a light drag setting, should have conductivity equal to quality drift rods, should have a 14-inch handle below the reel and some handle above, should have enough guides to distribute line over the J'ing area, and should have action crafted to distribute evenly into the butt.

In addition to finding a rod in the Shakespeare cupboard, I also found that Fenwick had a rod in inventory that fit the downriggers' needs. A steelhead rod, the FS83, and its spinning cousin, the FS83C, it was brought out of the closet on the Pacific Slope by steelheaders who'd gone downrigging. Buzz Ramsey, professional fisherman for Luhr Jensen, handed an FS83 to me while we were on the Deschutes River chasing steelhead.

"But this is the rod we had aboard your downrigger boat," I said.

"Right on," Ramsey said, and proceeded to demonstrate versatility by hooking a sucker instead of a steelhead.

Later I found that the rod that meets all of my downrigger rod specifications for mini-rigging, Great Lakes downrigging, and light saltwater downrigging is also a good surf rod. It's 8¼ feet and casts ¼-to ⅝-ounce lures on 6- to 15-pound-test line. It has a fast action with the upper 33 inches bending and torques the same J length. It torques down with the drag on a light setting—particularly needful in mini-rigging. The handle below the reel seat is 14 inches, with plenty of cork above the reel. The rod, designed by Jim Green, Fenwick's chief rod designer, for reading steelhead drifts, has great conductivity. The casting version mates well with a President II, 1984, in surf, on drift, and on downriggers.

The Eagle Claw closet also held steelhead rods that downriggers began using. Eagle Claw now markets two that meet my specifications—the 8½-foot GHCD 429 and the 8-foot, 2-inch PRCU 829. Both have the same action, with the rod torquing at the 35-inch mark. Also Eagle Claw's 7½-foot SECM 423 is a good rod for handling the large Chinook of the Inside Passage or for light saltwater use. Designed by Bud Eastburn, a Pacific northwest fisherman, the rod has heavy-duty guides and reel seat. A stiff rod with the action in the upper 33 inches, it torques to a high drag setting and should not be used for bluegill fishing.

The flyrod closet also held a number of blanks that were crafted into good downrigger rods. Don Gundling, owner of the Rod Makers Shoppe near Cleveland, handcrafts downrigger rods from Shakespeare tarpon flyrod Ugly Stik blanks. He customizes the tips of these blanks to customer needs. At the Canadian Fenwick plant the 9010 flyrod blank was crafted into the Rigger Rod. The Rigger Rod started in an exciting way. Downrigger fishermen on both sides of Lake Ontario discovered the rod simultaneously and began driving to the Canadian plant to get blanks. Dick Gaumer, public relations director for Fenwick-American, visited the plant, noticed the customers, and met with them to find out their specifications. Rumors among fishermen have it that he redesigned the blank by cutting off the tip. "Not true," Gaumer says. If produced for the American market, the rod will be 9 feet long with white finish and will be called the FL108-10, Don Gundling says.

Fenwick will also offer the DR82 in both casting and spinning versions. It will have a slightly heavier action than the Rigger Rod.

One of the special problems that downrigger captains face is that their rods get banged around. The rods are in competition with downrigger booms; charter captains have customers who, in their excitement, give the rod hard usage; and rods have to be piled into cabin space for storage after fishing. The Ugly Stik brings special strength to solve that problem. The name was given when during early experiments with epoxy resins, Shakespeare workers obtained an ugly green color, Bob Hipp, Shakespeare executive, explains.

"Later, as we made the rod in graphite with its special tip, the nickname came to stand for strength," Hipp says. The rod tip gives good torquing and conductivity without great production expense by a marriage between an epoxy rod and the hollow graphite-content blank. "A strand of graphite or boron extends from the hollow section up into the epoxy most of the way to the tip," Hipp explains. The action and torque of the rod extend from the tip end of the epoxy rod well into the graphite hollow blank. Because graphite has great dampening ability, the rod dampens well. The handle works well in downrigger rod holders. The 9-foot and 7-foot light-action BWD 1101 and 1131 torque down to lighter drag settings than the 7-foot medium-action BWD 1120. Although conductivity is not as super as in a hand-crafted rod, it rates high because graphite has super conductivity. Shakespeare also offers a fiberglass 8½-foot downrigger rod, Honey Stik BWD 1400.

Skyline in Fort Worth is supplying Southern bass, hybrid bass, striper, and ocean downriggers with rods, including an 8-foot rod that is high in graphite content and works well for light ocean fishing.

Rigging down with 6- or 8-pound-test line can be done with a 10- to 11-foot noodle rod, the Surf Rod, made by Dick Swan, Clare, Michigan, rodmaker and guide. The rod has eighteen guides. "If the drag's set down with 15-pound line, a big fish could break the rod," Swan warns. This slow-action rod will torque into a U shape on a light drag setting. After pop-up the fisherman retorques a Swan rod by pointing the butt cap at the fish. The bend of the rod whips the fish.

The cry "Fish on!" points to a mystery shrouded in water. The mystery the fisherman seeks to solve is: How solidly is the fish hooked, and what will be its angle of fight? The fisherman has already learned something about the mystery from seeing the rod tip flip upward, and from looking at the line. He knows how deeply he's set. He knows how he's rigged—whether he has a dodger, at what length from the release, with what lures. He probably has some idea of the species taking. As the fisherman takes the rod, he's "feeling" for more information. The rod should be taken out of the rod holder with a high, upsweeping motion.

The fisherman should not sock the hooks to the fish. While sweeping upward to take out slack, the fisherman should be feeling for the fish to determine its position in the water and its weight. Immediately after pop-up, there will usually be some slack line between rod tip and fish. This occurs because of a corner the fishing line makes (shown at A in Figures 4 and 18) when torqued down. That right angle will become an arc after the line releases. Of course, frisky fish, including Chinook and steelhead, may take that slack out. Some fish sound as they hit so there isn't a pop-up. Instead the rod tip is immediately forced downward by the sounding fish. But this is unusual. On downriggers most fish set the hook adequately themselves. The pull to free the line from the release, the forward trolling force of the boat, and, to some extent, the upstroke of the rod tip all combine together for good setting in the majority of cases. Most fish follow the lead of the trolling boat for a short time after they hit. The fight begins as the fisherman puts tension on the line. He wants to know whether the fish is large, is swimming along with the direction of troll, has already turned away, is about to sound, or may be about to leap. None of these situations is helped by taking out slack with a strong-muscled sock-it-to-'em hook-setting action. (Muskie usually are an exception!) Instead, lift the rod with controlled power to let the fish work against the limber tip. This puts the fisherman into a position that allows his rod to forgive his errors.

The fish may tear the water off the mystery very quickly. Sails may race past the boat. Chinook, steelhead, bass, and sails may leap out of the water. Other fish, including Chinook, channel cats, and bottomfish, may sound and sulk. Unless the fish is sighted in the air, the information comes by vibration up the line and through the rod tip. The fisherman's finger and arm muscles must be educated to know these signals, and the best helper is a rod tip that transmits them well. One reason my fingers and arms respond so well to my FS83 is that I'm on the steelhead riffles with it in winter and early spring. It's wise to buy a good rod that your muscles and nerves like.

Deep-sea rods for large sails, marlin, big sharks, and any ocean fish that may go several hundred pounds escape one of the criteria of downrigger rods. The tips can't be torqued into a C shape. They're too stiff. With them, line angle and tension between tip and release are the primary clues to below-the-surface fish behavior. Norm Newman uses Fenwick IGFA, Fenglas rods for large ocean fish. Captain Rubins uses them for the deep waters of Lake Tahoe.

It's not fun to fight fish on heavy line. And if you've paid for a rod crafted to let you feel the muscles of the fish, why equip it with line that

Charter Captain Skeeter Rubins holds a Fenwick rod that meets IGFA ocean trophy specs. Set with a Penn 349 reel, it takes big lakers at depths over 100 feet. (Courtesy Skeeter Rubins.)

dampens the feeling? Line of 8- 10- and 12-pound-test is reasonable for inland lake and light saltwater fishing, though 20-pound-test line is consistently used by charter boat captains who have to deal with an assortment of customers who may be in various conditions of sobriety. But the charter boat captain who's watching for trade from outdoorsmen usually has a few reels equipped with light line. "Here's a rod set up just for you," Captain Torba frequently says, and he'll watch to see whether the customer sizes the line with his finger tips.

The first trolling reel I used from downrigger fishing was my bass-plug and big-river-steelhead reel—a level-wind Pflueger Supreme, No. 1573. Because it doesn't have either a star drag or a free-spool lever, the handle has to be snubbed with a rubber band to keep the line from paying out between the release and the tip while trolling. Slide the rubber band up the rod handle, twist once to a figure-eight, and loop over the lower handle. When raising the rod, the thumb of the hand under the reel flips the rubber band off. (It's nonsense to say that the fish will break the rubber band.) The same thumb will get blisters if a steelhead or Chinook takes off. The next trolling reel I got was a Shakespeare President II, and a 1984 is nuzzling the "antique" Pflueger beside the typewriter as this is being written. The President II replaced the Pflueger because the rubber band can be a nuisance, because a larger spool with greater line capacity is needed, because crank turns should multiply spool turns, and because a star drag that can be easily adjusted while fighting a fish is essential. Other trolling reels that meet these specifications include Penn's Levelmatics and Senators, and Garcia's Ambassadeur series. There are many others.

I learned how to play fish from catching Atlantic salmon, Chinook, and steelhead on flyrods equipped with free-spooling reels with good drags. In the stream the initial drag setting is just strong enough to make the spool engage when cranking in a rigged line against the current. Everyone forgets that some drag is obtained from the turn of the line over the tip line guide. That's a fulcrum—a pulley with no wheel—and that plus friction in the other guides is enough initial drag. There are two reasons for this. First, a light drag prevents breaking off when a fish strikes hard. Second, a fish that mouthed the lure (most takes are like that) will usually swim sedately against a light drag, and this gives the fisherman time to get ready for leaps, hard runs, and other maneuvers. These stream essentials apply when aboard a boat. So start with a light drag and turn it down when the fish is ready. The drag should be tightened slightly as the fish tires, perhaps loosened as the fish nears the boat where it may be frightened by the net. Those who adjust their drag while fighting fish must teach their thumbs and fingers how to turn the controls. Slowly increase drag against pay-out. Do not snub!

The first spinning reel I used also came from a steelhead rod—a Zebco,

Cardinal 4. It's still on one of my downrigger rods. The Cardinal 6 holds more line; the 7 has a higher retrieve ratio. These open-face reels have heavy-duty worm gears. That's essential when trolling in fresh water or salt. Because spinning reels are manufactured for a higher range of light-duty uses than trolling reels, it's important to check the quality of the gears. Some manufactured for light-duty Sunday-afternoon pursuits have soft gears.

The boat can be used to help fight large fish. If the fish has taken most of the line, the boat can chase the fish and help the fisherman retrieve line. If the fish is about to run under the boat and foul the line, the boat can be moved. When sailfish or other fleet species threaten to outrun the boat, evasive action can be taken. But a boat can only help a rod and reel. It can never apply leverage or engage in direct combat with a fish. If a captain is trolling near bottom or over jagged habitat, he may not want to put the engines in neutral for average fish. When the boat is in neutral, lines settle toward bottom. If one is fighting a fish while slow trolling, the boat may be going two miles per hour. The fish is fighting that thrust, and the rod tip is absorbing some of the force. At such times it's best to turn the boat so the fish is at 45 degrees from the transom. Then the fish can be played in an arc and not in the direct line of trolling force.

The greatest thrill is to hook a large fish under the threat of storm clouds rising from the horizon. Then one must fight both the elements and the fish. One evening in early August, I was trolling for Chinook with Captain Torba out of New Buffalo, Michigan. There was a storm coming up, but we were not far from the harbor. It was almost dark and the water reflected the angry color of the sky. We started to lift the lines, and as I approached the fourth downrigger to break the line loose from the release, the rod took a sudden, savage dip toward water.

"God, it's got to be a big one," Torba said.

I could already feel the size of the fish, which was swimming downward and out to sea. It continued to take line and to follow the bottom contour, which sloped toward mid-lake. Overhead we heard thunder. Torba was frowning at the turbulence, and the wind, which had mostly been aloft, now hit the outriggers with a fury.

"We've got to get that fish fast," Torba said.

I said in a pleading voice, "I could break off." I might as well have said, "Please, don't make me break off." Meanwhile the fish did little to tire itself, and line had payed off enough to show the reel arbor in the gloom. Torba put the engines in gear and ran forward while I reeled. A few raindrops hit the cabin. After Torba heard my signal—"Enough line gained"—he came back with a flashlight so we could watch the line on the reel. He'd positioned the boat at 45 degrees from the fish's course. Now it sulked.

I beat the rod butt against the gunwale, but these vibrations had no effect on the fish. I heaved up against the weight of the fish, bending the rod alarmingly. This did no good. It was now raining hard; the wind took my cap, and the boat was pitching over the rising waves. In the gloom, whitecaps could be seen reflecting their ominous warning.

"Get that fish moving," Torba said.

I took all pressure off and stripped line from the reel to give the fish a sense of freedom. Then Torba started slowly toward the light on the harbor breakwall. It worked. The fish allowed itself to be led, and after a slow wave-tossed run of several thousand feet punctuated by blots of lightning that caused Torba to grumble, the fish came up to the surface.

"The line's come up, sir," I said.

"Then make the fish leap," Torba said. He put the engine into neutral. "I'll have to turn the boat into the wind," he said. He put the engine back into gear.

As I put pressure on the fish, I saw the most glorious sight of my outdoor career. A bolt of lightning illuminated the fish's leap. Then, as the rain increased, the fish ran straight for the harbor light and leaped twice more. Although it was still "green," I was able to pump the fish to the boat, and Torba, leaning over the gunwale with a flashlight tucked between his chin and his chest, netting it. It was 29 inches long and weighed 30 pounds, 4 ounces.

The more a fish runs, the sooner it will tire. The fisherman should encourage running and leaping. Fish don't have large hearts, and it's hard for them to work their gills when they're swimming hard and leaping. They'll soon run out of oxygen if exercised. One time we were out with a novice who had never played large fish. He hooked an Atlantic salmon from a canoe and insisted that the guide let him play it slowly. It took an hour and a half to land an 11-pound fish. Sheer nonsense!

Many fish, like the one caught in the storm, can be led on a line like a sheep on a rope. Lou Black, who taught me how to troll for Atlantic salmon, demonstrated this in the George River. It was dangerous to play the leapers from a canoe, so we'd troll until we got a strike. Then Lou would turn the canoe toward shore and slowly, gently lead the trout to land, where he'd get out and put the pressure to the fish to signal the beginning of the contest. The fish usually leaped, then ran.

After a fish is hooked, it should be allowed to run as far as it likes on a loose drag. This is particularly feasible if one is in a boat on open water with no nearby boats. Of course, if the space has been invaded by other boats, runs may have to be slowed, if possible, by tightening the drag.

Each fight is different. Once Stan Lievense and I took a Chinook in Lake Huron out of Harrisville. Lievense had the rod, and the fish took off in a burst of speed, turned, ran back to the boat, and sulked beneath it. Lievense reeled as fast as he could and got all the slack line out of the water. The fish, lying at 50 feet, conserved its energy, and Lievense couldn't discover any way to budge it.

"He'll get back all the energy he lost in that run," Lievense said.

I moved the boat to a position about 100 feet from where the fish had sounded. Then Lievense took all tension off, letting the line go slack in the water. The fish came to surface some distance from us, but sounded again when Lievense put on the pressure. Again I moved the boat and Lievense put on pressure. Again the fish rose and sounded. We tried to lead it on a light line, but this didn't work. "He's going to break off," Lievense said. I put the boat into neutral, and Lievense pulled line off the reel.

"I'm sweating," Lievense said. It was nearly noon. On land people were sweltering under an August sun. Lievense gave the rod to me, and ate a sandwich and drank a beer. I kept pressure on without moving the fish.

"It's not stuck on the bottom," Lievense said. He took the rod and put it in a rod holder, letting the line go slack. Before long we saw the line moving up in the water, and the fish surfaced and leaped about 300 yards behind the boat. Lievense had folded his arms, but when the fish started a run over the surface, he grabbed the rod. In another ten minutes I netted the fish, an 18-pounder. A light rein will often move a sulking fish. It's better to put the rod down than to break off.

When fighting strong fish on light tackle, always remember to maintain correct position during every tiring moment of the struggle. Correct position is having the rod tip up, to let the fish work against that, and pointed toward the fish, so it won't make a right angle and break off. Furthermore, during every moment of the fight the angler must look toward the fish. This helps one to keep lined up in correct position and to keep an eye on the line. And it allows one to anticipate the moment of leaps. When a fish leaps, it's best to give some slack—to "bow" to the fish, a bend of the knees or a courtly bow from the waist. This is especially important when one is close to the fish or in a small boat that's low to the water.

When a fish tires and can be brought to the net, do not tighten the drag and crank the weight through the resisting water. Instead, pump the fish, then reel up the slack line you gained. Pumping the fish will water-ski him over the surface if he's on his side.

Not all netting can be successful, because fish do wear holes that allow the hook to unhook. But a little care will make most nettings into happy experiences. Don't use a short-handled net when there are many obstacles such as downriggers or outboard engines or if the boat is high above the water. An 8-foot handle will save many fish from being tangled. Many captains carry nets of two different handle lengths. A rubber band that keeps the net against the net handle will save some tangles. Finally, remember to move the fish over a sunken net so that the man handling the net can lift the fish without having to poke the net at it. The fish should be moved over the net as it is pumped in toward the boat in a continuous line of force. Stopping the fish, then starting the weight again is not a good tactic. Sometimes the fisherman must back toward the stern as the fish comes in over the net, and the netter must give careful instructions, because the backing fisherman loses sight of the fish.

Fish that are large enough to be clubbed should be hit halfway between the nose and the eyes. If they're struck too far back, they may bleed profusely from the gills. During fishing contests, this loss of body weight could be costly.

Charter Captain Terry Walsh shows good form as he raises net over transom while Bob Boughner backs toward cockpit to keep line from fouling. (Courtesy Michigan Travel Commission.)

12
Salmon Trolling in the Salt

This book is written from the Great Lakes downrigger's convictions that fish usually seek habitat by temperature preference, that the habitat can be located with a thermometer, that the fish can be located within the temperature habitat with sonar, and that they can be caught on lures presented by a downrigger. This method was developed while fishing for salmonids imported into the Great Lakes from many parts of the world. Three of them—Chinook, coho, and steelhead—came from the near-shore water and tributary-river habitat of the Pacific Ocean. In 1978 I went to see whether Great Lakes methods would take these species in their native waters.

Before telling my adventures on the Pacific Slope, it would be best to make some comparisons between the "water physics" of these two habitats. The comparison is between a part of the native range of steelhead and salmon—the near-coastal salt waters of northern California, Oregon, and Washington—and the Great Lakes. These habitats differ sharply. Because of upwelling, the near-coastal salt waters of northern California, Oregon, and Washington do not follow the "rules" of the thermal stratification cycle as the Great Lakes waters do. Upwelling prevents near-coastal surface waters from warming in summer as they do in the Great Lakes and most other water bodies. Upwelling mixes the salt water from top to bottom, interrupting the summer establishment of thermal layers. During winter, spring, and fall, near-coastal Pacific waters from top to bottom range near the salmon temperature preferendum. Salmon can find much habitat throughout these waters. In summer also (a time when salmon in the Great Lakes have to move out of sun-warmed upper waters), intermittent upwelling keeps most of the water within the salmon preferendum. Off the coast of central Oregon, for example, early-summer surface temperatures often warm to 57 degrees. But by summer the operation of the upwelling system will reverse the sun's warming, causing surface water to be lowered by about 7 degrees. Upwelling also raises nutrients into the waters of the Pacific Slope for the nourishment of forage fish and creates food for salmon.

If the near-coastal waters of the Pacific Slope warmed in summer as the Great Lakes and most other water bodies do, a summer thermocline would form there and salmonids would migrate into it. Great Lakes waters have fairly well-defined temperature distinctions. The thermometer shows that in the Great Lakes it's much warmer near shore in the spring, that there are three temperature layers when the thermocline forms, and that it's warmer at the bottom in winter than at the near-frozen surface. But in the Pacific Slope upwelling region, the thermometer is not easily used. So upwelling, created by summer winds from the northwest, is an atypical force that creates an atypical environment—a unique ecological niche where salmon flourish. It makes summer trolling much easier off California, Oregon, and Washington than it is in the Great Lakes—easier because there are usually a few taking fish in these salt waters even when the northwest wind stops blowing, the waters warm, and the fish become lethargic. Even when the bite is off because the winds have changed, ocean trollers will pull their lures through remaining pockets of cold water. Summer upwelling, because it creates a continuous habitat within the salmon preferendum, often makes Great Lakes temperature hunting seem pointless. That's the reason why many Pacific Slope downriggers do not use thermometers. It's also the basis for the Pacific Slope myth that its waters do not vary in temperature from top to bottom.

There's a region north of Washington in the Inside Passage and along the coast of Alaska where salmon and steelhead flourish that doesn't experience an upwelling system. Would thermometers help find fish habitat there? I don't know. I haven't been there. Letters from biologists in that area indicate that trollers do not use thermometers to find fish. Instead they follow the forage fish. There may be good trolling in areas where fishermen do not know what the forage fish are doing. Some data indicate that Chinook are sometimes taken in very deep, cold parts of this water, but, apparently, sportfishermen have not put thermometers into this water. However, British Columbia fishermen, following the leadership of Saltaire Publishing, are fishing deep for salmon with Scotty Depthking downriggers. They report taking fish that netters overlook.

In addition to upwelling, there are two other factors that make the near-coastal waters of northern California, Oregon, and Washington different from Great Lakes water—the discharge of large rivers and large tides. The Columbia River plume, which extends toward the south in summer and toward the north in winter, complicates temperature fishing, especially near the lightship anchored near the Columbia River bar. Fish may be repelled by changes in temperature and turbidity caused by the river. The tides may, at certain times of day, drive forage fish out of areas of water that are at temperatures comfortable for fish.

Upwelling occurs when cold lower waters rise because warm upper waters were blown away. The water may not directly move in the direction the wind blows. On the Pacific Slope when the wind blows from the north the water moves seaward toward the west. This is called the Ekman Drift, and it occurs because the wind blowing toward the equator combines with the rotation of the earth and frictional forces to send the water at right angles. A narrow current flows in the same direction as the wind along the seaward side of the front, and a deep current flows in the opposite direction. Fishermen can detect upwelling by observing the wind, the surface currents, and the major discolorations in the water caused by the raising of tiny marine plants and animals that attract forage and game fish. On a summer day when a strong northerly wind blows along the Oregon coast, fishermen look for a line in the sea where clear cobalt blue changes to murky green. There they catch salmon, tuna, and other species. They are fishing where cooling waters have increased game fish metabolism and concentrated forage fish! Screaming birds wheeling above the color line echo the fishermen's cries of triumph.

When the summer northerly winds die and southerly winds rise to blow warm upper water back toward shore, water temperatures may rise, causing fish metabolism to fall. Furthermore, the fish may have "fed up" and may fast for a while as they become dormant in warming waters. Sonar may show the presence of fish in the warming waters, but they may not take. "The bite is off," fishermen will say. It may be useless to continue trolling through these fish. At such times, trollers should use their thermometers to search for pockets of cold water that still exist. These pockets may last longer at lower depths because warmer water being blown back into the habitat floats on the colder water. This is particularly true within the influence of the Columbia River plume, which extends into the sea for many miles.

Spot upwelling can occur in any water body. Good places to look for spot upwelling include eddies around the lees of islands or land promontories jutting into currents, ridges, and above canyons. In the open ocean, upwelling occurs near the equator and in the Antarctic. But the upwelling we've been discussing is a large system occurring off coastal areas in the low and middle latitudes in North America, South America, and Africa. The Pacific Coast system occurs along the coast of Baja California, California, Oregon, and Washington near the California Current. Upwelling there moves up the coast in warming weather in May, June, and July as the North Pacific high-pressure cell strengthens and northerly winds flow along the coast. It's over by October.

Upwelling is intermittent. When the Pacific prevailing wind stops blowing in the direction of the equator and stops the transport of offshore water, the upward circulation of cold water stops. The southerly wind that blows warm water back toward the shore is not circulating water. It is simply pushing floating surface water. So there is not a reverse upwelling influence. When mixing stops, nutrients are no longer raised or mixed into upper waters, the growth of phytoplankton stops, forage fish and game fish disperse. The entire system collapses. Trolling becomes counterproductive. At this time it's best to hunt with a trolling thermometer for pockets of cold water.

I have detailed a few of the forces operating in the near-coastal waters of one ocean. There are not so many forces at work in the Great Lakes and smaller inland lakes and impoundments. Oceans have gigantic surfaces swept by wind, long areas for formation of waves, many kinds of waves, tides, permanent currents, and currents that form because of wind action. And while all these variables are operating, the seasonal thermal stratification cycle is ongoing. Remember that the upwelling systems are interruptions in the wind's mixing of the sun's energies. What does this mean for the troller? It means that he's towing his lures through all kinds of forces that he can't see, may not know anything about, and may have difficulty observing. The fish feel these forces and are affected by them. For these reasons, downrigger trollers are wise to study the waters they fish. This study will bring fishermen into conversation with biologists and oceanographers. And there are many barriers in communication between these three groups. The wise ocean downrigger will form clubs to which biologists and oceanographers can be invited for educational lectures, and he'll form his own bull session within this club. There's little point in burning gasoline and buying complex gear unless you know a lot about the water your propeller is disturbing.

When scientists assembled all ocean variables to report to Oregon coho fishermen in 1973, catches skyrocketed. Daily, weather permitting, June through August, a single-engine Cessna gathered data for Oregon state oceanographers. Air data included surface temperatures, location of upwelling, water fronts, color changes, birds, fish, and fishing boats. Oceanographers prepared a sea surface temperature map over a known ocean topographical map. The twenty-four-hour prediction map stressed the location of 52- to 56-degree water and predicted concentration points for coho. Copies of maps were sent to the Pacific City Dory fleet and Newport and Depoe Bay fishermen's radios. Fishermen using the forecasts found coho present in good number at prediction points, particularly on days when major oceanographic changes occurred. For those days, the catch doubled for recommended points over other points. This project, covering Cape Lookout, Oregon, to Seal Rock, demonstrates two things. First, all variables should be gathered together. Second, temperature is a major variable in predicting daily fish habitat location. Fishermen highly praised two advantages the reporting gave them. They knew where to start and wasted little time finding the fish. When 52- to 56-degree water was known to be two to three hours from port, they went out and caught fish—without the certainty of the forecast they would have turned back.

I didn't know anything about upwelling when I met Buzz Ramsey, Luhr Jensen's promotion manager, at the docks in Chinook, Washington, in July, 1978.

"Our bite is off," Captain Ramsey said. "The north wind that usually cools our upper water has stopped."

As Ramsey headed the 23-foot Glas ply Luhr Jensen research boat into the channel to the Columbia River, I looked over the Auto-Trac downriggers. Two electric short-arms were mounted on the stern gunwale. Manual long-arms with double hand cranks and flip-slip brakes were mounted on the starboard and port gunwales. Ramsey saw me eyeing the double cranks—the first I'd seen.

"Raise the weights with both hands or either hand?"

"You got it," Ramsey said.

Although we "got the skunk out of the box" with two small "silvers"—coho—the bite stayed off during that first day of nonproductive trolling. That night Ramsey took counsel with Dick Seine, a second-generation commercial fisherman who trolls with lures. (Most Western commercial and many sports trollers use bait.) Seine, captain of the *Sonja*, had done much better—three coho and two large Chinook.

"Tomorrow, leave on the flood tide and start at a point 2 miles beyond the lightship on a 180-degree course from the south jetty," Seine advised.

Ramsey consulted *Tidegraph,* a tidechart, and learned that the flood tide would begin at 5:00 a.m. He groaned.

"Unreal!" he said.

Jensen research boat being readied for trailering to Chinook, Washington. From Chinook, the research team runs the channel to the Columbia River mouth, then across the bar—an alarming passage—to the Pacific.

At 5:30 a.m. we navigated the hazardous channel from Chinook to the Columbia River channel. We'd seen a boat aground in the channel the previous day. Ramsey guided our boat over the bar where the river and ocean waters meet and set a 180-degree course. As we crossed the red line, the buoys marking the south side of the channel, we saw the beacon on the lightship that marks the beginning of the red line. Fog now reduced visibility to about 5 miles. The ocean had gentle swells. There was no chop except at the bar, where Ramsey had some slight difficulty with side chop. By 7:00 we had Seine's *Sonja* in sight at a point about 2 miles southeast of the lightship. The high wooden outrigger poles on the green wooden craft built in 1928 made a distinctive silhouette.

"Glad you made it," Seine said on the CB. He had already taken a 3-pound silver and a 5-pound Chinook.

Successful passage over the Columbia River bar is always cause for thanksgiving. Even fishermen who cross it twice daily as Seine does are glad the passage is over. Ramsey had a coffee break while I set the stern downriggers at 24 feet with green and mother-of-pearl Tom Macs, the side riggers with Kelly green size 003 Tom Mack dodgers leading

Twinkle Squids (Seine's winning combination) at 20 feet.

Because of the north and south jetties, the Columbia River bar no longer has dangerous shoaling sand at every point where tide and river water meet. However, at extreme low tides, shoals emerge. Other hazards exist. At flood tide, the smoothest time to cross, a northwest-to-northeast wind can combine with incoming water to set disabled craft onto Clatsop Spit. Winds form the south or the west can sweep disabled craft onto the North Jetty or Jetty A farther within the river mouth. At ebb tide, waves may build to hazardous heights as incoming ocean waves are opposed by outgoing fresh water and ebb tide. An even more dangerous butting of these waters occurs on minus tides when A-frame waves are formed. This condition is not easily visible to the novice approaching from the Columbia River. After Ramsey went back to Hood River, I hitch-hiked with a first-year commercial fisherman and his wife in a 60-foot retired naval craft. The wife started coffee water boiling in the galley as we approached the bar. A few minutes later we were in the A-frame-shaped waves and the coffee water flew off the stove. In addition, every other object in the boat went through the air, including me. The boat labored up the waves too slowly and descended too fast. Sweat broke out on the captain's face. His wife became physically ill. While our captain fought for control, two other craft turned sideways in the trough of waves and capsized. One sank. No one drowned. Immediately after we cleared the bar, we were in relatively calm water. Then our engines quit. We were in mortal terror because we thought waves would take us back into the turbulence, but the Columbia River current swept us seaward across Buoy 3, where the Coast Guard cutter reached us.

Navigation to the bar is made hazardous by sands that frequently shift the Illwaco and Chinook channel courses. The boat we saw aground was following the channel marker, but the sands had shifted, making the marking erroneous. The captain, who couldn't have known about the shift from reading his chart, could have avoided the danger by using a depth finder. His condition wasn't serious. He went aground at 1:00 p.m. on the ebb and was floated off again at 6:00 by the rising flood tide. But he and his passengers had an uncomfortable five-hour wait in a crowded, canted boat. Captains navigating the Columbia River mouth should frequently check their depth finders. They should also avoid leaving the marked channel to cut across at the North Jetty. It's unsafe to leave the channel to cut north between Buoy 7 and 9 because one's craft is likely to go aground on Peacock Spit where breakers occur. It's also unsafe to cross the red line to cut south between Buoy 12 and 14 because one is likely to go aground on Clatsop Spit. Fifteen minutes after flood tide is reversed,

Salmon Trolling in the Salt

Clatsop Spit can be covered by breakers that will wreck grounded craft.

These are the reasons Ramsey and I were saying our Sabbath thanksgivings as we set lines.

"I hope the bite is on," Ramsey said. Holding a wetted finger up, he noted that the south wind was still blowing. His marine radio had predicted a shift in winds. "We need our north wind," he said.

But the bite stayed off. The wind didn't change. We trolled south, then north. The cormorants, gulls, and ball ducks flew with us, but neither birds nor man found fish. Seine came on the air, saying, "Set at 40 feet and stay there for a while." He'd taken two more small silvers at that depth. Ramsey explained that silvers in that area are usually taken in the upper water. "They must have gone down to find cooler water," he said.

At 9:00 we had a double on the stern rods set at 40 feet over 60-foot depth. Two silvers weighing about 3 pounds took gold Hot Shots. The boat stayed on course while captain and mate played the fish very carefully. The stern electrics came up at the press of a button. I cranked one manual left-handed; Ramsey took the other. We each netted our own fish. "If we get close together the fish we've both got on will get tangled," Ramsey advised.

Ramsey radioed Seine: "Our skunk is out of the box."

But, despite zigzagging and figure-eighting, fish that showed on sonar refused hotshots, Tom Macks, dodger/Twinkle Squid combinations, J-Plugs, and Fishbacks. We trolled south; Seine trolled north. Nothing. At 10:00 we pulled the lines and ran down to the south jetty to fish within 100 feet of it.

"Jellyfish hole," Ramsey called it, because we'd seen many large yellow jellyfish there the day before. They were still there. Some of them were as large as a medicine ball, and they frequently fouled our lines and down weights. We knocked them loose with the gaff.

At the jellyfish hole, ball ducks amused us with their continuous taxi. They hold their wings up to create an airfoil, which lifts their body weight out of the water but leaves their legs dangling, ankle deep. Their webbed feet tread the water, moving them forward over the swells. They don't heel-and-toe over the surface. They tread. They don't lift their feet to the surface. Their feet go around and around in the water, impelling them forward. To stop, they fold their wings. To lift into flight, they flap their wings.

We pulled the lines and went through the channel on a 300-degree heading, crossing the black line at Buoy 3. From a distance we'd seen birds circling that area. As we neared the birds, Ramsey spotted a rip.

I saw an area of calm water about 2,000 yards long that looked like a gigantic Atlantic salmon lie. At the edge of this slick there were whirlpools, ripples, floating weeds, planking, rope ends, and other debris. "The temperature will be several degrees colder on the ripple side," Ramsey said. We set all lines at 10 feet with small J-Plugs, and Ramsey steered to keep the port lines in the turbulent water, the hull in the calm water. We immediately took two silvers and lost them in a line tangle. On a second pass we took two more and put them in the box. Ramsey was disappointed because we didn't take any more.

"It's a good rip, but *all* the water's too warm."

We pulled the lines and headed in. While we were stowing gear, a rain began that obscured the coastline. We ran on a heading of 40 degrees and scanned the horizon for the lightship beacon. Somehow we ran through the black line without seeing it, but we picked up the red line and headed toward Chinook. While we were making passage, the wind changed. We had the boat hoisted out and put onto the trailer.

"North wind tonight," the hoist man said.

The next day we limited in two hours on Chinook biting super-large J-Plugs. The bite was on!

There's another saltwater body where Pacific salmon flourish that isn't subject to upwelling or large river-current influence—Puget Sound. It's more like the Great Lakes. Dave Davis, executive director of the Les Davis Tackle Company, took me trolling there.

The Les Davis research boat, Bang Tail.

My wife and I met Captain Davis on a Sunday at his dockage in Commencement Bay in Tacoma. The tide was out and the ramp from the parking lot to the dock sloped sharply downward. Mussels were left high and dry on the green barnacle-encrusted mooring posts. I hauled my heavy camera bag along the dock past a commercial fishing boat named *Toil*. The black-lettered word "Toil" on white trim reminded me of Adam's banishment. But as we boarded Davis' new boat, the *Bang Tail*, we returned to Eden.

The *Bang Tail*, named after the Scalelite-dressed spinner, is a Bayliner created in the yacht division of the Arlington, Washington, yards to Davis' specifications. It's 35 feet long and 13 feet 1 inch wide. It has a bridge that seats five people comfortably, two bedrooms, a bathroom, a kitchen with two refrigerators and an icemaker, and a combination wheelhouse and stateroom. The captain can steer beside the dining table in the stateroom or from the bridge. Powerful twin gasoline engines purr at the slowest required trolling speed. Davis himself tunes them. The transom is correctly arranged for downriggers, and there's adequate room in the stern area just outside the stateroom for tending lines and fighting fish. As we moved away from the dock, Davis turned on the electricity and water. My wife said, "This will be a style troll!" We made a short cruise over smooth waters to Point Defiance. The gigantic eddy there was one of Davis' childhood fishing spots. His Point Defiance lure takes its name from the spot. It's also the place where Stan Lievense, then an enlisted navy man on leave from his ship docked in Tacoma, caught his first salmon. Point Defiance is at the intersection of three arms of the sound—Colvos Passage, the Narrows (Tacoma's Narrows Bridge cross it), and Dalco Passage, which leads to Commencement Bay, where Davis docks.

Davis decided to fish with sinker releases because the downriggers hadn't yet been installed on the *Bang Tail*'s transoms. We put out three lines. The port quarter rod was rigged with a No. 1 Les Davis Herring Dodger, a No. 4 Point Defiance flutter spoon dressed with green Scalelite, and a round 20-ounce sinker. We let out about 150 feet of monofilament. Davis found bottom by bouncing the sinker up and down and reeled up a few feet. The starboard quarter rod was rigged with a No. 1 chrome dodger dressed with green Scalelite, a No. 6 Point Defiance spoon dressed with silver Scalelite, and a round 16-ounce weight. The stern rod placed between the quarter rods trolled a Phosphorglow green Witch Doctor and a round 8-ounce weight.

Sound fishermen can troll year-round for salmon. The native population decimated by urban stress is gradually being rebuilt. "This state program gives good fishing November through December—perhaps better fishing in winter than summer," Davis explained. Many salmon spawned in streams tributary to the sound used to run out to sea to be netted by northern netters. New species have been planted that turn left and run to California, where they're safe from commercial netters. Originally, some salmon remained in the sound year-round, but most of these strains have been fished out. The state now releases smolt later than the stream out-migration time. These are the fish caught in winter. Forage for them is primarily herring and candlefish.

A Sunday armada of boats of all sizes was already trolling and mooching near the Point Defiance eddy when we arrived. Several fishermen had taken large kings. Our trolling route was from Point Defiance across Dalco Passage to Point Dalco and back. We made this trip in an elliptical pattern while tracing our way among small boats. My suggestion that we anchor and preach to the fleet was ignored. It was a perfect opportunity to advertise Les Davis lures, but the *Bang Tail* doesn't have a sign on it. "Might advertise our mistakes," Davis said. He prefers a yachting atmosphere.

Rips formed by the tidal currents flowing through the three passageways formed appropriate trolling targets. They made large pond-shaped slicks, and we put out flat lines to troll them. At 8:00 a.m. the tide became an out-tide and boats drifted in dispersion from the point into Dalco Passage. This improved action for moochers who took many dogfish, some silvers, and a few big kings. The out-tide created difficulty for trollers. Davis had to run his RPM up occasionally and turn the wheel against currents to keep course.

Our weighted lines ran fairly well but sometimes fouled other boats' lines, the bottom, and big kelp. We saw several yellow jellyfish, but jellyfish line fouling was less frequent than in the ocean. We were the largest ship afloat, but we weren't laughed at or cursed. People whose lines we fouled worked patiently with us. They backed their boats toward the tangles and held their rods patiently while Davis made urbane apologies. Many people recognized him and gave him a friendly greeting. On one occasion we worked with two other boats, an orange Bayliner and a white Glas ply, to create and uncreate a gigantic line tangle. No lures were lost!

We fought bottom, backed down to bottom where our lines sometimes fouled, and felt for bottom with our weights. "We may bottom out before the stock market," Davis said.

Until we rigged flat lines to troll the slicks, the fish didn't bother us much. Then three small silvers took. The fish were polite. Each of us got a hit. Davis netted all fish, including his own, which turned out to be the largest—about 3 pounds. All took Point Defiance spoons.

13
New Saltwater Frontiers

This is a chapter about downrigging in salt water for species other than members of the salmonid family. Downrigger sales to ocean trollers are increasing, but we do not have enough experience with temperature fishing in the ocean to be able to know what methods will mold the sport. Some ocean species run deep, requiring a thermometer to find their habitat and a downrigger to present lures to them. However, in many parts of the ocean there are often abundant species at the surface the year round. In waters off Baja California, for example, blue marlin may move out during winter, but black marlin move in. So among the many surface species using Baja waters, there's always one present that likes the temperature. This means that although temperature habitat is just as important to surface fish, thermometers are not as important to surface fishermen. Fish inhabiting surface temperature habitat are in an obvious place. Some resistance to temperature fishing arises from saltwater fishermen who think that preferendums mean that there's a magic temperature at which a member of a species must bite. There is not, and a species may exhibit one range of temperature comfort in one geographical region, another in some other region. So ocean preferendums may not always be regionally accurate. Somewhere on the ocean, a downrigger fisherman is trolling for solutions to these problems and many others.

Norm Newman, professional fisherman for Riviera, does not use a thermometer as much for ocean fishing as he does for Great Lakes and other

A 47-pound sailfish. (Courtesy Norm Newman.)

inland lake fishing. "Temperature is as important to the fish as in fresh water," he says, "but it's not as important to the *hunting*. You can often find the species you want by following the fleet or fishing the known areas." He still relies on downriggers—"The best trolling tool," he says—and sonar—"My eyes!"

In the early days of Great Lakes salmon fishing Newman built his own downriggers out of washing-machine pulleys. A resident of Paw Paw, Michigan, he was active in Michigan Steelheaders, and served as one of the first presidents of the organization. Jim Rieth, president of Riviera, needed help developing his marine and tackle business. He had a burden with the tool and die side of the company, so in 1974 he invited Newman to take over field promotion and downrigger testing. Rieth gave Newman a magnificent fishing assignment: "Wander the lakes and oceans of America with downriggers." He made Newman the captain of a center-console 25-foot Mako, the *Riviera I*.

Rieth's assignment, supported by increasing profits from Riviera downrigger sales, gave Newman the time and equipment to become a far-ranging, pioneering downrigger fisherman. He's now working to improve the use of downriggers in salt water. He's fished in the Gulf, the Pacific, the Atlantic, and out of the Keys. The preferendum chart (see Figure 23) he's developed from interviewing biologists and from his own fishing experiences are among the first for downrigger ocean fishing. He's extensively tested rods and reels for ocean downrigger fishing. For

New Saltwater Frontiers

	Saltwater Preferendum	
	MOST ACTIVE	DISTANCE BEHIND WEIGHT
Barracuda	64°-67°	20'-60'
Bluefish	66°-72°	10'-40'
Cod, Atlantic	44°-49°	20'-40'
Dolphin	73°-77°	20'-60'
Marlin, black	75°-79°	40'-60'
Marlin, blue	77°-80°	40'-60'
Marlin, striped	68°-72°	60'-70'
Marlin, white	70°-78°	60'-70'
Sailfish	76°-81°	60'-70'
Striped bass	45°-65°	40'-60'
Swordfish	64°-68°	60'-150'
Tuna, bluefin	61°-67°	50'-70'
Weakfish, common	68°-71°	20'-40'
Weakfish, spotted (seatrout)	70°-74°	20'-40'
Yellowtail, Pacific	64°-68°	60'-70'
Yellowfin Tuna	66°-72°	90'

Figure 23. *The Lievense rule applies:* When a species' ideal temperature is not available, the fish will seek the temperature closest to it. *Also remember that these temperatures are not magic numbers ensuring that fish will strike. After finding water of the preferred temperature and fish in the water, skilled presentation is still necessary. (Data gathered by Norm Newman, Field Promotion Manager, Riviera Marine and Tackle Company.)*

these reasons, and because my ocean fishing has been only in the Pacific Northwest, this next section on downrigger fishing for sailfish, snappers, and groupers is Newman's information.

Newman began by saying: "Jim Rieth, my boss, and I have tested a lot of equipment in Florida waters. I want to tell you about a super day we had down there when we took sails on downriggers set both shallow and deep.

"We went out of Duck Key in late November in windy weather with 4- to 5-foot waves," Newman said. "Jim got down to the dock at 7:30 a.m. He was wearing a swordfish cap and a short-sleeved shirt. The air temperature was about 72 degrees.

"'Captain, let's go after some sails,'" Jim said.

"I put the twin 175-horse Evinrudes into gear, and we headed east for about 8 miles to a coral shelf inside the Gulf Stream. The reef is at 45-foot depth, and it drops off to 90 feet on the Gulf Stream side. I'd already caught some ballyhoo for bait. We planned to troll them behind our downriggers instead of artificials. They're one of the forage fish sails like to eat.

"Jim was looking at the ballyhoo while we were running. 'Look like billfish,' he said.

"Ballyhoo—the real name is balao—are a forage fish found in most tropical seas. They have a long lower jaw that reminded Jim of the upper bill on sails and other billfish. We catch them in sunlight over dark patches—not light, sandy patches—of bottom. We put out a chum bag, wait for the fish to school in, and bag them with a cast net.

"As Jim and I arrived at the reef, the surface temperature gauge read 72 degrees. Jim dropped the Temptroll to 30-foot depth, and it was the same reading all the way down. This was a little cooler than it had been because of the east wind, which was blowing smartly across the reef. The prevailing wind down there is from the southwest.

Jim Rieth (in stern) and Norm Newman set the port downrigger on the Riviera I. The center-console Mako 25 is equipped with a Riviera Temptroll, foreground, and Simrad EY sonar, background. (Courtesy Norm Newman.)

"We set two lines on downriggers at 15 feet over 90-foot depth. We baited with live ballyhoo. When trolled slowly, they swim along with the boat. I hook them behind their long, lower jaw, all the way through, with the hook pointed in the direction of the troll. We set with 12-pound line, a Fenwick saltwater PLT 903 7½-foot rod, and a spinning reel. We also put out two flat lines rigged the same way. I had the Simrad EY sonar on, and I steered by the 90-foot contour. The bait was 60 to 70 feet back, and Jim was watching for sails following the bait.

"I find that sails are most active in 76- to 81-degree temperature," Newman explained, "but I was certain that we'd take fish in the 72-degree water we had. Sailfish are a billfish like marlin, spearfish, and swordfish. Ed Migdalski, the author of *Angler's Guide to Salt Water Game*

Fishes, says that the bills are found in areas where water temperatures don't fall below 59 degrees. He thinks they don't go to depths where the temperatures are below that. His habitat maps show them ranging from Point Conception, California, to Valparaiso, Chile, on the west side of the North and South American continents, and Key West to Mayport, Florida, on the east side. So, like most fish, their habitat is restricted by temperature.

"Jim Rieth was extremely interested in the new way I set the lines that day. I put a slack loop in the line between the rod tip and the release because of the way sailfish hit live bait. First they hit it to stun it; then they circle around and take it.

"'Great!' Jim said. 'This solves a big problem. When the sails hit, we'll let them mouth the bait for a while. Then when they run with the line we'll set the hook!'

"Rieth is a sharp fisherman, and I was glad to have his approval," Newman said.

"After guiding on the 100-foot contour for a long time, I called a couple of other boats in the area—the *Shakespeare,* captained by Arlin Leiby, and the *Coral Key,* captained by Billy Wagner. Action was slow for them, so I went into deeper water and guided on the 110-foot contour as it marked on the graph. We didn't set the lines any deeper. I heard Jim yell: 'Sail coming up!' The gigantic dorsal fin was cutting through the waves. It glistened blue in the sunlight. A beautiful sight! It hit the starboard flat line, then there was a pause. 'Fish on!' Rieth yelled. He had the rod, waiting. The line began to run out, and Rieth set hard. The fish took to the air. The sunlight was just right to show a thrilling mixture of blue, silver, and bronze as the fish rose. First, up came the bill, then the gills flaring—an eye staring at us over the gills—then the whole fish was in the air, fell back, came up again like it had fallen into a trampoline net, fell again, then raced with incredible speed past the boat, and was off.

"Jim was disappointed. 'Oh, what a shame!' he said. 'But what beauty—a thrilling blue streak!'

"We reset. I'd pulled everything. We put a new bait on the starboard line, and we set our 9-pound down weights at 8 feet, this time over 110-foot depth. On the sonar I could see plenty of bait fish. The surface temperature was still 72 degrees. Still a little chop with the boat undulating up and down. I was at the wheel about half an hour, and the starboard downrigger went off.

"On its second leap this sail tail-walked across the waves toward the boat, the line dangling from the hook in his mouth, then he went subsurface and roared past the boat at 90 miles per hour. I got on the wheel and angled out to take up the slack, then kicked the Evinrudes out of gear as the line tightened. Jim, walking around the console, went to the bow to fight the fish. I went to the stern and got the Temptroll and all the other lines up.

"The fish put on a terrific acrobatic performance. It must have leaped fifteen times, and Jim hollered every time it leaped. Then it sounded and sulked for about twenty minutes. Jim skillfully kept the pressure on through the 12-pound line, and the fish came to the surface. It leaped again, but Jim was gaining line, the fish was tiring. Jim worked his way back to the stern, I turned the boat to keep the fish at the stern, and Jim slowly pumped it up to the starboard side. I put on cotton gloves, grabbed the fish by the bill, got the hook out, and released it.

"Billing these fish can be dangerous. The bill is a club with a sandpaper surface and a sharp point on the end. The fish move that club at the end of their body with the accuracy of a golfer striking a golf ball. They can hit an 8-inch swimming baitfish with it. Migdalski reports seeing a boated marlin hit a crew member on the legs with its bill. Joe Brooks, in *Saltwater Game Fishing,* reports that two men have been killed while landing sails. Both were speared—one through the chest, the other through the neck. He and Migdalski report boats being damaged by the bills. Accidental contact with the rough part of the bill peels skin off—many people have had their chest, arms, or hands rasped when landing sails.

"We rerigged and started trolling again. I steered over the same area for about an hour, but nothing took, so we got out 20-pound tackle and dropped the down weights to the 90-foot depth to troll for groupers and mutton snappers. I put on 7-foot Fenwick PJB 847s and some trolling reels with the heavier line.

"The Temptroll at port showed the temperature still at 72 degrees at 90 feet. Rieth was just calling the reading off to me when the starboard rod released. The boss and I had a foot race to the rod. I won. Instead of reeling up in deep water, I often point the rod at the stern and set when the motor and boat pull the line taut. After I took care of that, Jim put the motors into neutral and got the other lines up. I could feel the fish heading for the rocks, but I got him turned and he came out fighting. I didn't know what species I had—something that works the bottom, but the graph hadn't showed many rocks, just a long, flat section of mud. After I worked the fish up I saw that it was a mutton snapper—about 11 pounds. Jim put on the gloves, grabbed the fish by the bottom lip, and pulled it aboard. We iced it for supper.

"We set again, and after a long troll the Temptroll went off. Jim did the honors on this one and landed a 6-pound yellowtail. As we put it onto the ice beside the mutton snapper, we could see that the mutton's seven dark vertical bars were fading. Both of the fish we had in the box were of the snapper family. The mutton was a pretty good size. Usually members of that species average about 4 to 6 pounds. Most snappers are bottomfish, but yellowtails may be found at middle depths. They're both game fish specializing in gigantic surges toward rocks where they hide, and we get into some real tugs of war with them.

"It was now 12:30 and time for sandwiches. We decided to troll west at right angles to the reef even though it meant raising the riggers as the depth decreased. We reset, and as I was watching Jim put the ham on the rye, bingo! off goes the port downrigger, which was set at 80 feet over 100-foot depth. Rieth's reflexes are quick. He dumped the sandwich into the cooler and got the rod. The fish came to the surface and leaped—a sail, and taken at that depth! As I was getting the lines out of the way another sail, perhaps 30 pounds, hit a flat line. I grabbed that rod, waited, hit him three times; then he leaped twice and was off.

"Jim still had his fish on. It took an hour and twenty minutes to get it in. It sulked a lot and tried to rest up, but Jim had charge all the way. The fish took to the air, and entertained us with acrobatics and beautiful colors. The runs that fish made were unreal—so fast! Jim handled the reel well. He kept enough tension on the fish to tire him but remained alert to the danger of breaking off.

"I billed the fish, and Jim looked him over. He had a happy expression on his face. All his corporate cares had drained away, and he said: 'Good boat handling, captain.' As you can imagine, that made my day.

"We figured the weight on this fish at 65 to 70 pounds. Sails of that poundage are probably in the last year of their life. We decided to boat this one and have it smoked. Smoked they taste delicious, and Jim wanted to fly some hors d'oeuvres back to Grand Rapids. He grabbed a pair of gloves and helped me haul the fish over the side.

"During the fight this fish had worked us toward the Gulf Stream. We decided to troll in the stream and set with 20-pound-test line at 70 feet over 90-foot depth. We had three live ballyhoo left, and I was hungry enough to eat one of them! I grabbed two sodas and some bread and meat out of the cooler. We just got our mouths full when the starboard downrigger went off. I grabbed the rod. Jim went to the wheel, then came dashing back when the port downrigger went off. We both had sounding fish. Jim's got caught on the bottom—probably under a rock. I put my rod in the holder and grabbed the wheel so I could hold the boat in the area of Jim's rock-snagged fish. He and the fish engaged in a tug of war, which Jim won. The fish was a 7-pound mutton snapper. After it was in the box, Jim put the boat into reverse and backed down to my fish. He had found his house in the rocks, and I had to give slack, wait a while, then strike him, and tug. I won and boated a 25-pound grouper.

"We were exhausted, so we headed in. I ran slowly until we'd eaten a few sandwiches; then I put the throttle down and we ran up to the dock, where we had our sailfish hoisted out. Four sails on, one killed; three snappers, and one grouper in the box. A good day for downriggers in the salt!"

In addition to taking sailfish at the surface, Newman and Rieth took one at 80 feet. Ralph Horton, editor of *Pennsylvania Fish 'N,* fishes deep with downriggers for bluefish and stripers in the Atlantic. He starts fishing for blues in early June off the Jersey coast. He finds stripers there in March, April, May, September, October, and November. The stripers don't like the Jersey coast midsummer warm water, so they go to Cape Cod in the last part of May and return in September.

Horton takes blues in water temperatures from 60 degrees and up. He takes stripers in 45-degree up to 55-degree water. He finds they move out when the temperatures go above 55 degrees. The blues take in depths from beachside to 80 feet. They feed on anchovies and on sand eels that they find at 70- to 80-foot depths. Stripers off the Jersey Coast and Cape Cod take at 20- to 30-foot depths and can be taken deeper, Horton says.

The downrigger technique pays off on black grouper. (Courtesy Norm Newman.)

New Saltwater Frontiers

For blues Horton uses surgical-tube lures; green is the most successful color. He says that blues will take many flashing, moving lures. He finds that it's good to present lures to stripers by trolling slowly and bouncing bottom. Bucktails, redhead jigs with a strip of pork rind, and squid imitations work well. Stripers will take a variety of slowly trolled plugs and spoons.

Downrigging in the salt is one of the new fishing frontiers. Ocean fishermen have found fish habitats through tradition. Sometimes they've used thermometers, but most of the fishing places in the ocean have been identified from colonial netting, Indian lore, and continued usage. From the point of view of the fish, these traditional "fishing holes" are temperature habitats. From the fisherman's point of view, they are hallowed places. We are just building a body of temperature data for the ocean. For this reason this chapter is an early report on a new frontier.

14
Mini-Rigging in Inland Lakes

In most inland lakes and impoundments, the temperature variables are the same as those that prevail in the Great Lakes region—the place where temperature fishing developed in partnership with downriggers. For this reason downriggers invented to troll for salmonids are used to troll for nearly all inland game species. Where the fish occur in small lakes and impoundments, downriggers are now often used by rowboat and bass-boat fishermen. The first trolling for bass, walleye, and northerns has, in most areas, been done out of larger boats of the Great Lakes—often by captains who started downrigging in pursuit of salmonids. So not all of the boats described in this chapter will be mini-boats. But there's an increasing trend toward mini-rigging out of rowboats in smaller lakes. The existence of this trend is underlined by the sales of downriggers for both small and large boats by Sears, Roebuck and Company. Sears' side riggers supplied by Big Jon have tapped gunwale mounting plates that can be attached to clamp mountings for rowboats. Most downrigger manufacturers produce small units that can be clamped onto rowboats or short-arm units that work well on transoms beside small outboard engines. Big Jon's Mini-Rigger is a clamp-on unit. Mac-Jac's Troll-Rite can be attached to rowboat seats for over-the-gunwale presentation. Riviera offers clamps that can be attached to the baseplates of several of their models. Luhr Jensen's Stantion-Gunwale Mount Bracket works well for side mounting on many small boats. Mike Lummis at Walker recommends the manual

Mini-Rigging in Inland Lakes

DT-2 for small or large boats. Nearly all manufacturers' short-arm units can be used on most rowboats and bass boats by installing diagonal plates for downrigger mounting bases at the corner where the starboard and port gunwales join the transom. Equipment for downrigging in inland lakes and impoundments of any size is easily available and extends the

The Harsen's Island Dory is a practical mini-rigging boat for inland lakes, rivers, and Big Water bays. It's 20 feet, 1 inch long with a 6-foot beam and an outboard motor well.

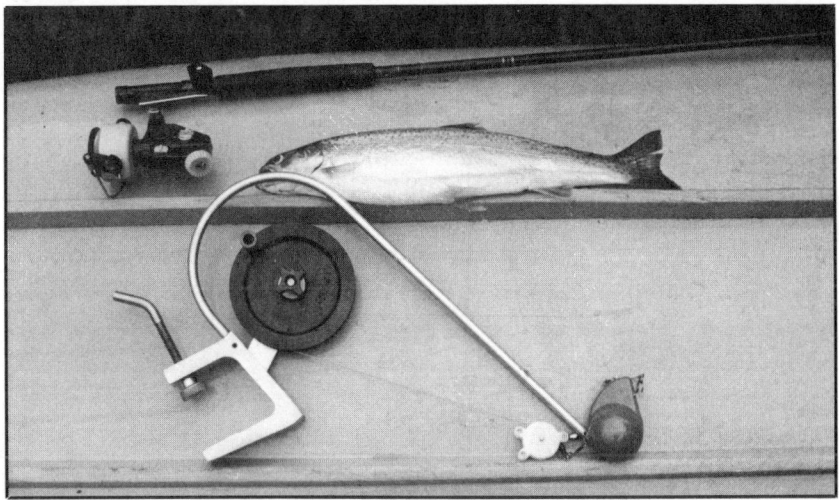

The Mini-Rigger that took the lure to this 20-inch rainbow has a 1½-pound down weight, a 4½-inch reel loaded with 75 feet of 50-pound-test cable, and a 16-inch boom. Reel is a Cardinal 4.

fisherman's ability to knowingly present lures to fish in their temperature habitat.

Fishermen on small inland lakes and impoundments are learning that fish take lures presented at controlled depths because they seek habitat in accord with temperature strata. I have taken bluegill, smallmouth bass, rainbows, and walleye with downriggers mounted on a 12-foot boat. In many states, stripers and hybrid bass are also being taken with downriggers on small boats. This may be America's fastest-growing fishing field. Muskellunge in the St. Lawrence River, the St. Clair River, and Presque Isle Bay at Erie, Pennsylvania, readily take downrigger-presented lures. Leslie R. Wedge, an aquatic biologist for New York, reports that fishermen on the Finger Lakes are downrigging in 14-foot boats. Fishermen observing me taking rainbows in Michigan's Shupac Lake went home to their workshops and returned with homemade downriggers fashioned from welding-wire spools and washing-machine pulleys. None of them knew that they were repeating the behavior of the Great Lakes downrigging pioneers. They only knew that they'd seen an improved trolling method, and they created the machinery to do the job. Probably nearly every American fisherman will soon have a pair of downriggers in his fishing-tackle closet.

Mini-Rigging for Rainbows

Trout lake rainbows explode from the water when taken on downriggers. A rainbow raised 42 feet of line set from my 12-foot boat to leap above the waters of Shupac Lake near Lovells, Michigan. The line was set at 32 feet with 10 feet behind the down weight. I saw the rod tip pop up and before I could get the butt out of the holder the fish was out of the water. I instantly reeled against slack, sensing that the fish was running toward the boat, but worrying that I'd lost it. In a few seconds I saw the fish on the surface about 2 feet from my white Johnson 3-horse. It leaped three times. Right beside the engine! I could have reached out to touch it. It got off!

The leaping reaction of rainbows to downrigger-presented lures presents split-second action, and I was at a disadvantage because I couldn't readily stand up to play the fish in the cramped space in my small boat. I lost the last seven rainbows I hooked on this trip, and they were all right in my lap, presenting an immediate excitement that I'd never experienced on larger boats. This 'bow was hooked with 8-pound-test line on a red Rebel Devil Crawdad presented on a 1½-pound down weight. Great action! More excitement than trolling out of a large boat, and with only a 3-horse gasoline bill!

Mini-Rigging in Inland Lakes

The green-and-brown camouflage-painted aluminum rowboat originally bought for duck-blind work has a narrow beam at transom (3 feet 8 inches, abruptly divided by the width of the 3-horse), which presented a downrigger-mounting problem. This was solved by mounting port and starboard Big Jon Mini-Riggers 2½ feet from the transom and a short-arm Luhr Jensen Auto Trac hand crank on the corner plate where the starboard gunwale intersects the transom. The Auto Trac had a counter; the Mini-Riggers payed out 11 inches of line for each counted turn of the mini cable pulley. The Auto Trac lifted a 6-pound Bonny-Invader down weight. The Mini-Riggers came equipped with 1½-pound weights, which proved unsatisfactory at depths below 18 feet because the cable planed out too far behind the boat when trolling. Two weights attached together remedied the problem.

A 22-inch rainbow taken on a Rebel Crawdad. In the foreground, a short-arm Luhr Jensen downrigger; in the background, a Big Jon Mini-Rigger.

My largest rainbow taken on the downriggers from Shupac Lake was 20 inches. After hitting a yellow Junior Flutter Devle, it became airborne, then ran under the boat. Alone in the boat, I wanted to lift downriggers. I got the motor shut off, crawled with rod tip held high to the middle part of the boat between the rowing seat and the rear seat, and stood up while the fish bulldogged beneath the boat. Using one hand for the rod, I got the port Mini-Rigger up before the fish, fortunately choosing that side, rocketed 15 feet out and leaped three times. There was a light wind, and my bulk acted as a sail that took the boat toward the fish, creating slack while I tried to use the net. I sat down, the net worked, and the fish flopped in the boat bottom.

The reason I crawled forward to play this 20-incher is that there isn't space enough at transom in this small boat to operate downriggers, engines, and rods and reel. Body movement in outboard-powered boats is usually blocked by the rear seat. It's designed for seated steering at the length of the outboard steering arm. It's a formidable barrier across the space between the rowing or midship seat and the transom. Some refitting is needed. The mechanics who copied my downriggers were already restyling their rowboats.

Being sailed willy-nilly before the wind is the biggest boat-handling problem I encounter with this light boat. The combined weight of the small outboard and the big person at the stern lifts the front three-quarters of the boat off the water, creating a pivot where the weight is centered. Any force—waves, wake from other boats, and wind—can make the boat yaw back and forth on its rear pivot. The thrust of the outboard at trolling and line-setting speeds won't overcome this yawing without continuous steering. This is particularly annoying when setting line. Alone, I must steer with my knees while setting with both hands. Button or doughnut-type releases pose the most difficult setting problems, because the button must be held in one hand while paying out line with the other. For this reason, snap-in releases such as Big Jon's Free'N easy, Al Ricker's Alligator Clip releases, and Walker and Riviera releases are better for small-boat usage. On large boats where the fisherman is standing and lures are paying off in water below his feet, it's easier to use button-type releases. Setting in a small boat is complicated by the fact that it's necessary to sit to the low-mounted downrigger cranks to operate them without pitching overboard. It's certainly different from walking around the broad base of the stern of a large downrigger boat. Taking a partner along to steer while setting is some help, but the person steering will be kneeling and reaching for the outboard handle to avoid adding his weight to the pivot point. Furthermore, his arms and legs will surround the man who's setting, giving him an octopus feeling.

After the lines are set, a mild wind can still be a dictating force in setting a trolling course. For example, when trolling against a starboard wind, the boat engine can be turned to hard starboard and carried by wind at a satisfactory troll to port. I have taken several fish on such courses.

In large boats, the engines may not troll slowly enough. The 3-horse in my 12-foot boat will troll so slowly that if a down weight catches, the cable will hold the boat motionless without strain.

Mini-Rigging in Inland Lakes

Women enjoy downrigger fishing too. In this photo, Joanne Haibach displays a dandy smallmouth bass.

When fishing alone, I would set the two rods legally allowed in Michigan with the Auto Trac at the starboard corner and the Mini-Rigger at the port gunwale. This gave a diagonal configuration that never created tangle either when setting or when making tight turns. When fishing with the one partner that boat room permits, four rods can be set. But they must be set with care on this narrow-beamed boat or tangles and line cutting in the propeller may occur. Usually three rods were set. A combination of long and short rods works best. The Auto Trac at the starboard corner was equipped with an 8¼-foot Fenwick FS83C. The starboard Mini-Rigger, when set, was equipped with an identical rod. The length was needed to get around the starboard corner line—particularly when setting. The port Mini-Rigger was set with a Shakespeare 7-foot Kwik Taper. The FS83Cs were equipped with Shakespeare President 1980 trolling-casting reels. The Kwik Taper was equipped with a Zebco Cardinal 4 spinning reel.

During mid-July of 1980, Shupac Lake temperatures ranged from 75 degrees to 41 degrees at depths of 55 to 65 feet. There was a thermocline. On most days, 50-degree temperature (the low range on the rainbow preferendum) was measured between 24 and 30 feet. The preferred temperature, 60 degrees, occurred between 19 and 24 feet on all ten days temperatures were recorded.

Lures that took fish included Rebel Crawdads and J-50 jointed minnows, flyrod Flatfish, Dardevle thin spoons, the Stanley Streamer, gold Luhr Jensen Hot Shots, and No. 2 Point Defiance spoons. Cowbells are used on Shupac Lake by flat-line trollers, but didn't do well for me. The J-50 takes browns, rainbows, and lakers for Ralph Horton, editor of *Pennsylvania Fish 'N,* when he downrigs in New Jersey's Round Valley Lake at depths from 15 to 70 feet. Horton also uses the J-50 for lakers in Chanute Lake at depths of 20 to 80 feet, depending on the season and temperature. The J-50 is 2½ inches long, the Point Defiance 1½ inches, the flyrod Flatfish 1¼ inches. Small lures are probably best in small, cold-water lakes.

The last fish I lost on Shupac Lake hit a new gold Hot Shot, leaped about 30 feet astern, then ran up to the boat and leaped three more times. I congratulated myself on maintaining control when the fish stopped leaping and peeled off 20 feet of line while running to starboard against the drag. It allowed itself to be reeled back, but gained energy and ran under the boat to leap far to port. It still seemed possible to land the fish, but it began to splash like an injured minnow on the surface about 15 feet to port. Feeling slack, I began to reel frantically and brought in a limp line end. The fish continued to splash on the surface—it was obviously tangled around the port Mini-Rigger cable. I raised the cable, and the fish, swimming on the surface, came toward the boat, but when the net was swung out it pulled free to swim away with the new lure.

Mini-Rigging for Bass

Ned Fogel, Michigan Department of Natural Resources biologist, had a special problem. He knew there were bass in a narrow, marl-banked Indiana lake, but the winding marl contours made it impossible for him to present a lure on a weighted flat line. When downrigges put the lures at the proper depth tight to the curving banks, he took fish. Fogel used a small rowboat powered with a 7-horse engine. After this success, he took trout and walleye in other small lakes.

Downrigging for Walleye

In western Lake Erie, walleye suspend and can be taken with downriggers, as Don Torba proved while chartering there during the summer of 1980. The custom in those waters is to troll flat lines or to cast weight-forward spinners baited with worms, so natives were astonished at Torba's Walker downriggers fished from his new 26-foot Henry Boat Works Skiffcraft. In the opposite end of Lake Erie at Erie, Pennsylvania, downrigging for walleye is an accepted custom, but isn't as much fun as downrigging for smallmouth.

Downrigging for Smallmouth

When the smallmouth popped up the tip of the Fenwick FS83C, Charter Captain Denny Harrington yelled, "Fish on!" and yanked the rod butt out of the Walker holder and handed it to me. I felt the fish surging to surface, where it leaped and fell back as I lowered the rod tip. "Big one!" Harrington yelled. It looked like a 5-pounder. The fish surging toward the boat came to the surface in a tail-skiing position with the Rebel Yellow Perch dangling from its mouth. During the rest of the fight it stayed underwater until taken aboard Harrington's Daymaker, where it weighed in at 4½ pounds.

We were fishing out of Jerry Sedney's Bayshore Marine in downtown Erie, Pennsylvania. We'd set at 15 feet over the 18-foot contour near the Sunoco Cribs east of the shipping channel from Presque Isle Bay into Lake Erie. Harrington steered the Daymaker by the 18-foot contour painted on his Lowrance LRG 1510B. Occasionally he zigged toward shore or zagged toward deeper water, but most of our fish came on this contour at 64 degrees set at 15 to 10 feet.

The strip of water we were fishing, which runs all the way to the New York line, is ideal smallmouth bass habitat. Presque Isle Bay, where Harrington docks, is ideal early-season habitat for Chinook and coho,

A smallmouth bass taken 15 feet down at 61 degrees over 20-foot depth.

and there's great muskie, smallmouth, and northern fishing in the bay, also. By midsummer, walleye can be taken on downriggers if fishermen can pass up the great Chinook and coho fishing that develops around "the mountain," an uplift in deep midlake. The salmon fishing improves as the fall runs come in, and some steelhead can be taken off the mouths of Elk and Walnut creeks.

Harrington, raised in nearby Fairview, started downrigging with a bass boat in 1977 after seeing advertisements in magazines. Using the ads for blueprints, he created his own downriggers from electric-dryer pulleys and window weights. Harrington had been fishing Presque Isle Bay and near-shore Lake Erie waters for years. He started in a rowboat off the mouths of Walnut and Elk creeks, graduated to a bass boat, then bought his 26-foot Reinelle powered by a Volvo PNTA. It was instantly clear to Harrington that controlled-depth fishing would solve many of the problems he'd encountered when using weighted flat lines. And from the beginning, his downrigging was for multi-species—both salmonids and nonanadromous fish. "From the time I got my charter license in 1979," Harrington said, "I've had as much business from walleye, muskie, and smallmouths as from salmon."

"The starboard downrigger is going to pop!" Harrington said. He rigs his sonar so he can see the starboard down weight, and he was watching a bass come up to the Bomber Firetiger. The bass was airborne in a few more seconds. Among the fifteen fish we landed and released that day, ten of them leaped. Smallmouth are nearly as lively as rainbows!

Downrigging for Muskie

Jim Beyers, Mount Clemens, Michigan, begins "hunting" muskellunge with downriggers shortly after they come off their spawning beds in Lake St. Clair and the St. Clair River. Beyers doesn't take temperatures because he's certain that he's always in muskie habitat and because he feels that this water temperature doesn't vary greatly. Setting at a maximum depth of 20 feet, he trolls large lures that require firm-gripping releases. "Walkers hold tight for me," he says.

Most of the lures Beyers uses were created by Charter Captain Homer LeBlanc, author of *Muskie Fishing Fact and Fancy*. His lures, created for setting hooks in the muskellunge's "snap-trap" mouth, are now being used for many species. They are a plug, the Swim Whizz; a spoon, the Swim Zag; and a spinner, the 4-B. "Our hardest-pulling lure is the Swim Whizz," Jim Beyers says. "It's 10 inches long and very wide. Looks like a parrot going through the water, and I really take a lot of muskies on it." (In Presque Isle Bay, Captain Harrington uses large Rapalas on downriggers for muskie.)

Although LeBlanc trolls for salmon with downriggers, he doesn't use them for muskie. He takes most of his muskies within 6 feet of the surface. "Seems like muskies won't take a lure much when our electronic gear shows them 15 to 18 feet deep," he says. But Burt Myers, editor of *Ontario Out of Doors,* has put downriggers on his boat because his larger muskies are taken below 10-foot depth. "While most muskie are taken from the top 6 feet of a lake, almost all of my bigger fish are taken below the 10-foot mark," Myers said in the February 1980 issue of his magazine. Jim Beyers feels that there are two advantages to trolling top water with a downrigger. "First, I know where I've put my lures," he says. "No guesstimating! Second, it's an advantage in the weedy waters I troll to have the down weight cable cutting a path for my lure."

Mini-Rigging for Striper and Hybrid Bass

Downriggering in temperature habitat for walleye, bass, stripers, and hybrid bass is a fast-growing sport in the South and Southwest. Joe Hughes, director of public relations for the Rebel lure company, fishes for walleye in Greer's Ferry Lake north of Little Rock, for striper and bass in Tenkiller Lake in eastern Oklahoma, and for stripers in Kerr Reservoir near Tulsa and Lake Maumelle near Little Rock. His sophisticated 18-foot

Eight- and 9-pound stripers taken in Lake Maumelle. A Fenwick rod and Garcia Ambassadeur 7000 reel work to the Riviera downrigger on the port stern. (Courtesy Norm Newman.)

bass boat is outfitted with temperature, oxygen, and light-meter gauges. He uses the thermometer the most. "If anyone asks me to isolate my most important piece of gear, the thermometer is it," he says.

Hughes advises rowboat fishermen using small downriggers to use plenty of weight. "Even when I'm fishing shallow I want to eliminate cable belly," he said, "so I put the maximum weight I can into my Riviera torpedo." He finds that grip-type releases work well for small fish. "I've taken 1½-pound Kentucky spotted bass on the Riviera release," he says. He feels that short-arm downriggers equipped with counters are the answer for the rowboat or bass-boat fisherman.

Hughes fishes Greer's Ferry Lake in October for white bass. "When threadfin shad come to the sun-warmed surface in the early morning, white bass may feed so voraciously that the water turns red with blood," Hughes says. "I've taken friends fishing who were so shocked when first seeing this mass of cannibalistic feeders that they couldn't cast. It's a shocking sight!"

As the sun rises, the blood-letting ceases as white bass descend to 20- or 30-foot depth. "That's when the downriggers come into play," Hughes explains. Lakes and impoundments in Hughes' region have a thermocline in summer often at a depth of about 30 feet—sometimes at depths of 22 feet. When they're deep, stripers usually are taken in 30 to 35 feet of water at temperatures of 60 to 65 degrees, Hughes reports. In lakes having a river channel such as Greer's Ferry, stripers may be deeper, often at 60 feet.

Fishing lakes of smaller acreage than one of the Great Lakes does not mean that smaller downriggers are needed. Small downriggers have their role. They are lightweight equipment to be carried along for switching to downrigging from water skiing or from other kinds of fishing. But short-arm, full-crank-size downriggers with counters are best for prolonged fishing on small-acreage lakes. Remember that shallow depth does not mean we should use smaller downriggers, that small lakes are often very deep, that heavy weights best prevent cable belly at trolling speed even when fished at shallow depth, and that counters are helpful because one takes temperature first, then lowers to a temperature depth.

Bass boats and rowboats are an advantage on a smaller lake. Short-boom downriggers balance well with them. But rowboats should be redesigned for mini-rigging. The rear steering seat should be removed to make room at the transom, and a steering wheel should be installed between the middle and the bow. This will shift weight forward, and increase tension on the outboard turning shaft. With these changes some standing in the boat can be tolerated. However, because standing in small boats endangers the person and makes him into a sail, he will often be kneeling to operate low-mounted downriggers. For this reason, the floor should be carpeted. Finally, some decking at the bow even in short boats will increase seaworthiness.

The same downriggers can be used for the fisherman's big-water and small-water boats. Ralph Horton has base plates on both of his boats, and he simply switches the riggers from his bass boat when he wants to go out on the Atlantic.

Conclusion

Successful downrigging is a practice—practice of a set of methods that leads to a bag of skills. The trolling trinity—downrigger, thermometer, and sonar—are the tools of the practice. Because this book sets forth a specific methodology that unites several fields, it's possible to believe that step 1 plus step 2 will result in a net miraculously filled with fish like the one cast on "the other side of the boat" in ancient Galilee. Such is not

Outboard at the pierhead light, Frankfort, Lake Michigan. (Courtesy Michigan Travel Commission.)

Mini-Rigging in Inland Lakes

the case. Each of the tools from each of the fields requires patience and practice. Reading sonar is an interpretive skill. Presenting lures is a fishing skill. Navigating large water or small requires seamanship. And the bottom line is that even when you limit out, each of the small number of fish you've caught will have had its own way of living out the preferendums and behavior patterns attributed to the mass of fish.

Because fish frequently change their behavior, everything said here is a guideline—a rule of thumb. Don Christenson says, "We are experts in the fishing business; therefore we feel it safe to say: 'We don't know what the hell they're going to do today!'" Bruce DeShano says, "Don't get locked into any one method. Constant innovation takes fish." DeShano is not recommending guesswork or trail-and-error. He knows the guidelines of downrigger fishing. They provide a baseline for his creative innovations. He does his fishing by using preferendums, color-penetration principles, sonar information, and temperature data as starting points. "Sure I want to know the temperature and the color of the lures, so I know what I spun off from," he says. "That way I'm not just wheeling and dealing. But it's innovation that takes each individual fish."

Roger to that!

Bibliography

Brooks, Joe. *Saltwater Game Fishing.* New York: Harper & Row, Publishers, Inc., 1968.

Christman, Skip. *Seeing Your Underwater World.* Vexilar Videosonar.

Clemens, Dale P. *Fiberglass Rod Making.* Tulsa: Winchester Press, 1974.

———. *Advanced Custom Rod Building.* Tulsa: Winchester Press, 1978.

Elman, Robert. *Fisherman's Field Guide to Freshwater & Saltwater Game Fish of North America.* New York: Alfred A. Knopf, Inc., 1977.

Figley, William. *Biochemical Monitoring of New Jersey's Nearshore Ocean Waters,* June 1967 to June 1978. New Jersey Dept. of Env. Protection, Div. of Fish, Game, and Shellfisheries Tech. Report No. 42M.

Harris, Walter. *Salmon Fishing in Alaska How & Where.* London: Thomas Yoseloff Ltd., 1940.

Harvey, J. G. *Atmosphere and Ocean, Our Fluid Environments.* Sussex: Artemis Press, 1976.

Hughes, Lawrence A. "The Temperature Cycle of Lake Michigan 1. (Spring and Summer), 2. (Fall)." NOAA Tech. Memo NWS CR-41, U.S. Dept. of Commerce, Natl. Oceanic & Atmospheric Adm., Natl. Weather Service.

Hutchinson, A. O. *A Treatise on Limnology.* 2 vols. New York: John Wiley & Sons, Inc., 1957.

Huyer, Adriana. "Seasonal Variation in Temperature, Salinity, & Density over the Continental Shelf of Oregon," *Limnology and Oceanography,* Vol. 22, No. 3 (May 1977), pp. 442–53.

Kammeraad, James. "Downrigger Trolling." Unpublished manuscript written for K-Line Industries, Inc., Holland Michigan.

Keller, Edwin H. "Color Perception of Fish," *Sportsfishing,* June 1973.

Bibliography

Kinney, Jo Ann S.; Luria, S. M.; and Weitzman, Donald O. "Visibility of Colors Underwater," *Journal of the Optical Society of America*, Vol. 57, No. 6 (June 1967), pp. 802–09.

Krauss, Robert W. *The Marine Plant Biomass of the Pacific Northwest Coast* (especially chapter 3, "Physical Characteristics of Pacific Northwestern Coastal Waters," by Adriana Huyer and Robert L. Smith). Corvallis: Oregon State University Press.

Lievense, Stan. "Catching Great Lakes Salmon & Trout." Mich. Dept. of Natural Resources, Inf. & Ed. Div.

Lowrance, Inc. *New Guide to the Fun of Electronic Fishing.* Lowrance Expert Anglers Series. Tulsa: Lowrance Electronics, Inc., 1975.

Maxwell, Jim. "Aquatic Acoustics & Sportsfishing." Fishing Tackle Tips Booklets, Grizzly, Inc., Vancouver, Washington.

Migdalski, Edward C. *Angler's Guide to the Salt Water Game Fishes, Atlantic and Pacific.* Ronald Press, 1958.

National Science Foundation. "The Sea Turns Over," *Mosaic*, Vol. 5, No. 1 (Winter 1974), p. 25.

Olson, Fred. *Exciter Fishing.* Tulsa: Winchester Press, 1978.

Packard, G. L. "Some Oceanographic Characteristics of the Larger Inlets of Southeastern Alaska," *Journal of Fisheries Research Board of Canada*, Vol. 24 (1977), pp. 1475–1506.

Radio Tech. Commission. *How to Use Your Marine Radiotelephone.* Radio Tech. Commission for Marine Services, P.O. Box 19087, Washington, D.C. 20036.

Royer, T. C. "Seasonal Variations of Waters in the Northern Gulf of Alaska," *Deep-Sea Research*, Vol. 22 (1975), pp 403–16.

Schumacher, J. P.; Kinder, T. H.; Pashinski, D. J.; and Charnell, R. L. "A Structural Front over the Continental Shelf of the Eastern Bering Sea," *Journal of Physical Oceanography*, Vol. 9 (1979), pp. 79–87.

Smith, Susan E., "Changes in Saltwater Angling Methods & Gear in California," *Marine Fisheries Review*, September 1979, pp. 32–44.

Squire, James L. Jr., and Smith, Susan E. *Angler's Guide to the U.S. Pacific Coast Marine Fish, Fishing Grounds, and Facilities.* U.S. Dept. of Commerce National Marine Fisheries Serivce, 1977.

Thompson, Harvey, W. *The Spooners.* Dearborn, Mich.: Eppinger Manufacturing Co., 1979.

Walford, Lionel A., and Wicklund, Robert I. *Serial Atlas of the Marine Environment: Monthly Sea Temperature Structure from the Florida Keys to Cape Cod.* American Geographical Society, 1968.

Index

A
Abe & Al flasher, 95-96
Adjustable release, 77-78
Alewife, 29, 87
Alligator-clip release, 70, 71, 146
Amplitude modulation (AM), 9
Andy Reeker, 107
Angler's Guide to Salt Water Game Fishes, 136-137
Aquatic wiggle of lures, 105
Atlantic cod, 135
Atmosphere and Ocean: Our Fluid Environments, 40
Auto Trac release, 71, 145

B
Baby Cowbell, 96
Baby Gang, 96
Banana Family of lures, 105-106
Barracuda, 135
Barrel-and-clip release, 72
Bass-Oreno plug, 105
Bear Valley, 96
Beer Can, 96
Big Dip, 105
Big Doctor, 106
Big O, 106
Billfish, 135-140
Blue marlin, 135
Bluefin tuna, 135
Bluefish, 135
Bluegill, 29
Boat rods, 109
Bomber, 105

Brook trout, 29
Brown trout, 28, 41-42
Brown rainbow trout, 29
Burke SA-Mon plug, 105
Button release, 70-71, 72, 77-78

C
Canadian Flash, 96
Canadian Plug, 105
Cannonball-shaped down weights, 73
Catching Great Lake Salmon and Trout, 27, 103
Ceramic transducers, 50
Charter captain, 6
Chinook, 14, 28, 41-42, 88
Citizen's Band (CB) Radiotelephone, 9-10
Clatter Tadpolly, 108
Clubbing, 121
Coast Guard Auxiliary (CGA), 6
Coho, 14, 28, 41-42
Cold-blooded fish, 27-30
Color penetration, 99-105
Colorado blades, 96
Columbia River plume, 124
Communication with fleet, 6-11
Conductivity, 111-112
"Cone angle," 50-52
Cowbells, 96
Crank Bait Family of lures, 106
Crappie, 29
Currents, 40

Index

D
Dardevle, 106
Deep Diver Family of lures, 105
Deep-probing thermometer, 44
Deep-sea rods, 115-116
Depth and color
 penetration, 101-103
Diamond, 96
Dinner Table Spoon Family
 of lures, 106
Doc Shelton, 96
Dodgers, 95-96
Dolphin, 135
Doughnut release, 77-78
Down weights, shape of, 73
Downrigger, 60-78, 79-89
 counter, 60
 down weights, 60
 engines, 91
 fouling lines on turns, 94
 how to set, 61-63
 Indian City, 64, 66
 mounting, 78
 pulley assembly, 60
 release; see Releases
 Walker, 22
Downrigger rods, 110-111
"Downrigger Trolling," 68
Downrigging
 for muskie, 151
 for smallmouth bass, 149-151
 for walleye, 149-150
Drift-Fishing Family of lures, 106
"Drift sensitivity," 112

E
Echo transducers, 49
Ekman Drift, 124
Electroacoustic transducers, 49
Epilimnion, 32, 34, 35

F
False release, 108
Fat Rat, 106
Fiberglass Rod Making, 111
Figure-eight trolling pattern, 93
Fish
 cold-blooded, 27-30
 migrations of, 12-16
 warm-blooded, 27
Fish Hawk combination
 temperature and
 depth gauge, 43
Fishing, temperature, 24-45
Flasher, 95-96
 Abe & Al, 95-96
 Les David, 96
 Luhr Jensen, 96
 Martin Tackle, 96
 rotating, 95
 sonar, 47-49
Flat Fish, 105
Fluorescent colors
 for lures, 103-104
Ford Fender, 96
Free 'N easy, 65, 72, 78, 146

G
Giant Cowbell, 96
Giant Pikie, 105
Glo-Go, 106
Graph, 79-89
 sonar, 47-49
Grizzly trolling indicator, 90, 92
Gurdies, 64-65

H
Hand-held thermometer, 44, 45
Hell Bender, 105
Hertz (Hz), 9
Hitchhiker, 70
Hot 'N Tot, 106

Hot Shot, 106
Hybrid bass, mini-rigging
  for, 151-153
Hypolimnion, 33, 35

I
Ice-out in Lake Michigan, 17-24
Indian City downrigger, 64, 66
Isothermal, 32

J
Japan current, 39
J-ing, 111
Jitterbug, 105
Jointed Family of lures, 105
J-Plug, 105
Jumping Jack, 106
"Jump-layer," 34

K
Killer Diller, 108
Kilohertz (kHZ), 9
Knot meter speeds for lures, 93
K-O Wobbler, 107
Krocodile, 107

L
Lake trout, 14, 27, 30, 41, 68
Lake Michigan, ice-put in, 17-24
Largemouth bass, 29
Lazy Ike, 105
Les Davis flasher, 96
Light waves, 100-101
Limnology, 31
Little Abalure, 66
Little Cleo, 106
Little Doctor, 106
L-Lures, 108
Loco, 107
Lowering, 75
Lucky Louie, 105
Lucky Luhr, 105
Luhr Jensen flasher, 96

Luhr Jensen rudder release, 78
Lure
  aquatic wiggle in, 105
  Banana Family of, 105-106
  choice of, 99-108
  colors of, 99-105
  Crank Bait Family of, 106
  Deep Diver Family of, 105
  Dinner Table Spoon
    Family of, 106
  Drift-Fishing Family of, 106
  families of, 105-107
  fluorescent colors for, 103-104
  Jointed Family of, 105
  knot meter speeds for, 93
  Non-Dinner Table Spoon
    Family of, 106-107
  Pencil Family of, 105
  shape of, 105
  sonic, 108
  Surface Plug Family of, 105
  Thin Spoon Family of, 106
  unpainted, 104-105
  upside-down, 104-105

M
Mac-Jac button release, 66, 78
Magnetic release, 72
Magnetostrictive transducers, 50
Main Train, 96
Maintaining station, 42
Marine-band radiotelephone, 8-11
Marine-band VHF-FM, 9
Martin Tackle flashers, 96
Mayday signal, 11
Megahertz (MHz), 9
Migrations, fish, and trolling
  plans, 12-16
Mini-Rigger, 142, 145
Mini-rigging
  for bass, 149

Index

for hybrid bass, 151-153
in inland lakes, 142-155
for rainbows, 144-148
for striper, 151-153
Mounti, 96
Muskallunge, 29
Muskie, 68, 151
Mutton snapper, 138-139, 140

N
Netting, 120-121
Non-Dinner Table Spoon
  Family of lures, 106-107
Northern pike, 29

O
Ocean upwelling, 39
Oceanography, 31
Odd Ball, 96
Okie-Drifter, 106
Owner captain, 6

P
Pacific Slope upwelling, 43, 123, 125-130
Pacific yellowtail, 135
Pan signal, 11
Peanuts, 106
Pear-shaped down weights, 73
Pencil Family of lures, 105
Pennsylvania Fish 'N, 140
Pflueger Supreme, 117
Point Defiance, 107
Point habitat, 39-41
Preferendum, 27, 31, 133
  charts of, 27, 28, 135
Puget Sound, 130-132
Pulleys, 63-64

R
Radio communication with
  fleet, 6-11

Radiotelephone, 8
  CB, 9-10
  marine-band, 8-11
Rainbows, mini-rigging
  for, 144-148
Releases, 60, 68-70, 96-97
  adjustable, 77-78
  Alligator-Clip, 70, 71, 146
  Auto Trac, 71, 145
  barrel-and-clip, 72
  button, 70-71, 72, 77-78
  doughnut, 77-78
  false, 108
  Luhr Jensen rudder, 78
  Mac-Jac button, 78
  magnetic, 72
  Riviera, 78
  rubber-band, 69-70
Rigger Rod, 113
Rip, 40, 129-130, 132
Rip tides, 40
Riviera release, 78
Rod and reel fishing, 109-121
Rod tip telegraphing, 108
Rotating flasher, 95
Rudder release, 78

S
Sailboat speedometers, 92
Sailfish, 135-140
Salmon, 13, 28, 68, 122-132
Salt water fishing, 133-141
Salt Water Game Fishing, 138
Sculpin Sounder, 108
Sea Skees, 97
Seasonal thermal
  destratification, 33
Seasonal thermal stratification, 33
Security signal, 11
Seeing Your Underwater World,
  53, 56

Shakespeare Kwik Taper
  Wonderod, 110
"Side Riggers," 78
Sinker release/down weight
  combination, 69
Slicks, 40
Smallmouth bass, 29, 149-151
Smelt, 29
Sonar, 31, 51, 56
Sonar graphs and flashers, 46-59
"Sonar T," 46
"Sonar trolling," 46
Sonic lures, 108
Spar-X, 105
Spawning, trout, 85-86
Spectrum Fishing, 103
Speedometer, sailboat, 92
Speeds, knot meter, for lures, 93
Spinning reel, 117-118
Spot upwelling, 125
"Stackers," 60
Standard Cowbell, 96
Stanley Streamer, 105
Stantion-Gunwale Mount
  Bracket, 142
Steelhead, 28, 41-42
Streamlined down weights, 73
Striped bass, 135
Striped marlin, 135
Striper bass, 151-153
"Suggestions on Dodgers," 95
Summer condition, 32-33
Sun
  angle of, and color
    penetration, 102
  warming of water by, 33, 34
Sunlight, 100-101
Surf Rod, 114
Surface Plug Family of lures, 105
Surface thermometer, 39, 44, 45
Swordfish, 135

T
Tadpolly, 105-106
Tennessee Shad, 106
Temperature, water, 33-34, 41
Temperature fishing, 25-45
Temperature habitat of fish, 32
"Temperature slope," 34
Temptroll, 45
Thermal destratification,
  seasonal, 33
Thermal habitat in rivers, 41
Thermal pockets, 39
Thermal stratification, thermal, 33
Thermal Stratification
  Cycle, 31-35
Thermal Stratification Year, 35-39
Thermistor, 44
Thermocline, 33, 34-35, 36
Thermometer, 12, 25-45, 79-89
  deep-probing, 44
  hand-held, 44, 45
  surface, 39, 44, 45
Thermotropism, 27-30
Thin Spoon Family of lures, 106
Transducer
  ceramic, 50
  echo, 49
  electroacoustic, 49
  magnetostrictive, 50
  mounting, 58
  power of, 58
  sensitivity of, 58-59
"Troller Says Let Temperature
  Be Your Guide," 37
Trolling brakes, 91
Trolling indicator, Grizzly, 90, 92
Trolling lines, 61-62
Trolling pattern, figure-eight, 93
Trolling plans and fish
  migrations, 12-16
Trolling reel, 117

Trolling speed, 90, 91
Trolling-speed meters, 92
Trolling swath, 93
Trolling tactics 90-98
Trolling trinity, 79-89
Troll-Rite, 142
Trout spawning, 85-86

U
Ugly Stik, 113, 114
Ultraviolet rays, 103
Unpainted lures, 104-105
Upside-down lure, 104-105
Upwelling, 39, 84, 122-123, 124, 126
    ocean and Great Lakes, 39
    Pacific Slope, 43, 123, 125-130
    spot, 125

V
Very high frequency—frequency modulation (VHF-FM), 9

W
Walker downrigger, 22
Walker release, 66, 67
Walleye, 29, 149, 150
Warm-blooded fish, 27
Water temperature, 33-34, 41
White marlin, 135
"Wiggle, aquatic," of lures, 105
Willow leaf, 96
Wind mixing and water temperature, 33-34, 41
Winter condition, 32
Witch Doctor, 105

Y
Yellow perch, 29
Yellowfin tuna, 135
Yellowtail, 139